Little-known Leicestershire and Rutland

Bob Trubshaw

Heart of Albion Press

Previous publications by Bob Trubshaw:
All published by Heart of Albion Press

Leicestershire and Rutland Earth Mysteries series:
Holy wells and springs of Leicestershire and Rutland
Ancient crosses of Leicestershire and Rutland
Standing stones and mark stones of Leicestershire and Rutland
Good gargoyle guide - medieval church carvings in Leicestershire and Rutland
Putting things straight - aligned ancient sites in Leicestershire and Rutland

Other titles
The quest for the omphalos - finding the mystical middle of England
(with John Walbridge)
Dragon-slaying myths ancient and modern
Grimr's year

ISBN 1 872883 40 0

Printed in England by
DAR Printing, Leicester

Heart of Albion Press
2 Cross Hill Close, Wymeswold,
Loughborough, LE12 6UJ

Contents

Part 1

Part 2

Front cover illustration:
The Pilgrim Cross at Frisby on the Wreake (see Tour 2).

To PVB

Acknowledgements

This book is the result of many years actively searching out once-lost features and, more recently, of leading various groups of people around different localities. Grateful thanks are due to the many friends who have provided help and support, especially those whose company made the field work more enjoyable and rewarding.

At an early stage of my research Paul Devereux most kindly made available all his published articles on Leicestershire and also his unpublished correspondence from Andrew York; Clive Potter proved to be an excellent co-worker; Max Wade-Matthews aroused my interest in sepulchral effigies; Jill Bourne and Bob Jarrett have refined some of my more nebulous notions; and Paul Nix provided all the much-needed help regarding computers and their software.

Preface

This book is intended to provide inspiration for outings to some of the unjustly overlooked treasures of Leicestershire and Rutland. It is not possible to provide a complete guide to such places and emphasis has been given to those sites which have survived fairly intact or are otherwise exceptional in their own way. However, if the route between two 'first rank' places passes through other sites of lesser interest I have included a brief account.

In principle the best way to visit such places is by bicycle, although I have attempted to provide more-or-less complete round trips to allow those living too far away to compromise by driving to the starting place before changing to two wheels. However, limitations on time or personal fitness do not prevent the sites being visited by car, although care may be needed to park without causing an obstruction.

However, the instructions and sequence of sites need not be strictly followed and readers may prefer to combine places from two adjacent tours to fit in with their own convenience and interests.

Some directions are given in the text but it is assumed that the reader also has relevant 1:50,000 Ordnance Survey maps. All grid references are preceded by the relevant O.S. Landranger sheet number. No less than five sheets are needed to cover all the county - 128, 129, 130, 140 and 141.

I am acutely aware of the ultimate irony in publishing a book on 'little-known places' - that these places will now receive far more attention than previously. While this may be beneficial in making it clear that the sites are a valuable part of our heritage, there is a risk that landowners may consider such attention to be unwelcome. The onus is on *all* people using the information in this book to ensure that their presence is welcome and will not prejudice the reception for future visitors.

In particular, please note that many sites are on *private property*. It is in your interests, and - more importantly - the interests of those following after you, that permission is sought before attempting access. Above all, the Countryside Code must be followed at all times and the unwavering principle should be to 'Leave nothing but footsteps and take nothing but photographs'.

For well-understood reasons many churches are now kept locked. What is not understandable is when there is no information on where to obtain the key! The best way to overcome this unnecessary and frustrating problem is to obtain the latest issue of the diocesan directories as these give addresses for the clergy and churchwardens. The Diocese of Leicester does not, however, include Rutland as these churches are in the Diocese of Peterborough. Therefore, both directories may be needed. These are available in person or by post from the Diocesan offices in Leicester and Peterborough.

Diocese of Leicester
3/5 St Martin's East
Leicester
LE1 5FX

Telephone: 0116 262 7445

Diocese of Peterborough
The Palace
Peterborough
PE1 1YB

Telephone: 01733 64448

Another worthy companion would be Pevsner's guide to the churches of Leicestershire and Rutland (Penguin 1960) as it is beyond the scope of this book to include a description of church architecture. Less well-known, but invaluable in its own way, is *Inside churches - a guide to church furnishings* (The National Association of Decorative and Fine Arts Societies, 1989).

Looking at church carvings is much more rewarding if you remember to take along a pair of binoculars and, for the lofty heights of dimly-lit roofs, a high-powered torch.

Some recommendations on pubs are included although these are based only on personal experience. As this falls short of an exhaustive appraisal of all available places, I owe a sincere apology to all those landlords whose establishments have unjustly been overlooked. And I can only hope, as and when any of the recommended places change hands, that future publicans maintain the high standards of their predecessors.

Some readers will be surprised that, twenty years after decimalisation, I have used imperial measurements such as feet and yards. There are two reasons for this - we still retain the mile as the main unit of distance and it seems perverse to mix metres and miles. Secondly, it just does not seem right to be describing traditional monuments in millimetres. Even such phrases as 'just under a metre long' seem perverse when to all intents and purposes the object measures one yard. I hope younger readers - and not-so young readers who may pick this book up in a few decades time - will forgive me for this stubborn antiquarianism.

I have also avoided the christocentric medley of Latin and English which hides behind the abbreviations 'A.D.' and 'B.C.' in favour of 'CE' (Common Era) and 'BCE' (Before Common Era).

The origins of this book lie with a series of booklets published between 1990-92 and various field trips organised for the readers of *Mercian Mysteries* magazine. Although the introductory chapters to wells, crosses, stones and carvings remain in a similar format to the earlier booklets, the number of such sites described in this book is far more restricted.

Updated information on the county's holy wells, ancient crosses, standing stones and medieval carvings has been compiled as an easy to use gazetteer published on 3.5" PC discs suitable for use on IBM PCs running Microsoft Windows. The title is *Little-known Leicestershire and Rutland - the hypertext* and is published by Heart of Albion Press. This software contains many of the illustrations used in this book (except maps) and also includes some colour photographs. The text information is far greater in scope as the number of sites described (including lost ones) exceeds 200.

Glossary of architectural terms

This is but a brief synopsis of some frequently-used terms to aid those with little or no familiarity with the common features of medieval churches.

All churches have a **nave** where the congregation sit. To the east is usually a **chancel** where the altar is set up, perhaps separated from the nave by a **chancel screen or rood screen**. In the chancel there may be choir stalls, and perhaps a **sedilia** (stone seats for the clergy set in wall niches) and a **piscina** (a small basin set in the south wall where the vessels used for serving the Eucharist would be washed).

Most churches have a door in the south of the nave, probably with an external porch. Exceptionally the entrance is through the north - or Devil's - door, but more commonly the north door has been blocked up. The most unusual entrance now (although originally the norm) is from the west. This has usually been retained where there is a tower on the west of the nave and the entrance is through the base.

In the great majority of churches the nave proved to be too small and **aisles** were added. Typically, the north aisle is slightly older than the south one. Where the aisles meet the nave is a row of columns and arches, known as an **arcade**. The columns may be decorated around the top - the part known as the **capital**.

vii

Where the arches rise up from the top of the columns (the **arch springers**) there may be decorative faces. Side aisles may also have piscinas (see above) near where secondary altars were set up.

Larger churches were sometimes built with a **cruciform plan**. This meant that between the nave and chancel was a tower, with side chapels or **transepts** extending north and south. In just a few instances the nave was still extended with aisles, giving interiors of magnificent proportions.

Churches have often been reroofed many times. In many cases the only evidence for early roof structures are stone **corbels** set into the wall, originally intended to support the bases of the roof timbers. Such corbels may be decorated with grotesque faces. In the apex of the roof (or the centre of cross-beams) the wood may be carved into decorative **roof bosses**.

Doorways and windows may have faces on either side, forming decoration between the vertical sides and the arch (or 'hood') above. Faces in these positions are known as **hood stops** (although I rarely use this specialist terminology, normally saying that such faces are 'by the door' or 'on the doorway'). Tradition seems to require that one face is male and the other female, with depictions of kings and queens being the norm - although there are plenty of alternative depictions of grotesques and animals.

The term **gargoyle** is often thought to mean any grotesque carving but it has a more specific meaning. Strictly, gargoyles are the decorated but nevertheless functional stone channels which take the rain from the roofs of the nave or tower and throw it out, away from the walls.

One specialist term which crops up is **tympanum**. This is simply a panel of stone which fitted into the semi-circular arch above a Norman door. Invariably the ones which have survived are carved, with some excellent examples of the art of the period. In many cases the original doorway has long since gone and the tympanum can be found embedded into any suitable blank wall. Frequently they are now inside the church itself, protected from the effects of weathering.

Dating the styles of church buildings

Although I understand the reason for academic researchers in church carving now using terms such as 'pre-Conquest Romanesque' and 'post-Conquest Romanesque' I have opted to keep the traditional terms of 'Anglo-Saxon' and 'Norman'. Both these styles are characterised by a rather solid and substantial appearance, with doors and windows surmounted with round arches. These arches may be superbly decorated.

By the second half of the twelfth century a radical innovation dramatically changed the appearance of architecture. The rounded arches of Anglo-Saxon and Norman churches were superseded by the pointed arches of the Gothic. This in turn allowed larger windows, which were broken up by stone tracery. The Gothic style is subdivided into 'Early English', 'Decorated' and 'Perpendicular' phases, although this nomenclature is slightly flawed and recent books speak of 'Early Gothic', 'High Gothic' and 'Late Gothic', respectively. More-or-less consistently I have just stated 'thirteenth century', 'fourteenth century', etc. but this itself is vague as each of these styles overlaps the turn of the centuries!

The fifteenth century brought a fashion for letting more light into churches and often the nave was increased in height to allow a clerestory roof, that is, one with as many windows as possible along the sides. The sixteenth century saw some arched windows being replaced with ones that were square-topped.

However, the Renaissance soon brought a Classical revival, with its own styles of architecture, which was in turn followed by a nineteenth century interest in Gothic revival. At its worst this led to some excesses of Victorian bad taste, but in Leicestershire and Rutland the Gothic revival is generally represented by mediocrity and banality. Probably Pugin's restrained designs for Mount St Bernard Abbey are the best representation of the Gothic revival in the county; he was also behind the restoration of St Mary's, Wymeswold.

Above all, remember when looking at a church that the structure is the product of continuous repairs, restorations and rebuildings. Even a church which retains a fairly unblemished appearance from, say, the thirteenth or fourteenth centuries has merely been at the receiving end of a more subtle process of renewal than one which more visibly has suffered from over-enthusiastic 'restoration' or just the accretion of ever-more extensions and piece-meal major repairs. It is not the purpose of this book to guide the visitor with the unravelling of the often complex sequence which characterises the building of individual churches, but if one starts picking up on the clues the relevant 'detective work' can become both addictive and rewarding.

Part 1:

An introduction to

Holy wells

Wells and springs are regrettably an undervalued part of our heritage. They are frequently built over, culverted away, filled in with rubbish, or simply overgrown. Yet up until the introduction of piped water in the early part of the twentieth century, they were an everyday aspect of life - so much taken for granted that historical documents rarely record them.

As with all areas of Britain there are certain wells in Leicestershire and Rutland known as 'holy wells' and several dedicated to saints. Almost invariably such holy wells have the reputation for never running dry and it is simple to imagine that, in an age without piped water, such a dependable source of unpolluted water was treated with reverence. Many such wells are, in fact, what would now be called springs - water which naturally flows out at the surface. Only comparatively recently have rural communities dug deep holes to gain access to water supplies.

When we visit the sites of such springs it is worth considering that water has been flowing continuously since before mankind came. Our distant forbears undoubtedly felt such places worthy of the greatest respect. But this attitude has never really dwindled. The pagan worship of water deities survived many attempts at christian adoption or suppression. Previously the well had a guardian spirit; the Church gave it a guardian saint.

Nationally, the saints most associated with holy wells are Our Lady, St Ann and St Helen. In spite of what the Church would like us to think, wells dedicated to lady saints may have been sacred to goddesses which predate christianity. Indeed, the medieval cult of Our Lady can be seen as the re-introduction of a thinly-disguised pagan goddess. It is simple semantics for pagans and christians to be just as happy venerating Their Lady. Sacred waters are traditionally 'symbolic of the Great Mother, and associated with birth, the feminine principle, the universal womb, the *prima materia*, the waters of fertility and refreshment and the fountain of life.' [1]

Furthermore, Helen may have less to do with the conventional christian hagiographies than with the Celtic goddess Ellen who, in Irish literature, used to emerge periodically from the pagan Underworld. Springs, in popular belief, were regarded as points of contact with the Otherworld. Helen is also closely associated with ash trees and many wells are or were in close proximity to this type of tree, as is suggested by the place-name Ashwell. Helen has the distinction of having two days dedicated to her; 3rd May and 18th August. It is said that May and August were the months when holy wells were believed to have their most beneficial effect.

As will be readily seen from the examples in Leicestershire and Rutland, there are many wells attributed with impressive medicinal properties. Various attempts have been made to explain this - the iron in chalybeate (pronounced 'kal-ib-eate') wells may have been beneficial; more subtle traces of mineral or organic matter may have had a 'homeopathic' effect; or maybe it was just that enough faith in the efficacy of such waters was able to overcome psycho-somatic symptoms. The more cynical have observed that, where the sufferer is required to fully immerse in the waters, the act of having a bath may have itself been beneficial in an age when vermin such as lice and fleas were rife and personal hygiene was a luxury.

Recent work at the Chalice Well in Glastonbury, the hot springs at Bath and the highly-reputed healing well at Sancreed in Cornwall has shown an exceptionally high level of natural radioactivity; so far no comparable Geiger counts have been carried out for wells in the Midlands [2]. The subtle increase in energy may have a 'homeopathic' effect; perhaps by inducing a quiescent state of mind.

'Holywell' is a widespread place-name and is usually derived from the Old English *halig* (holy) and 'well'. Alternatively, the origin may be from the Old English for 'omen' (*hael*) because such wells were used for divination. The Cornish clergyman Richard Polwhele [3] wrote in the first decade of the nineteenth century that:

'From those streams and wells put into agitation after a ritual manners, our forefathers pretended to foretell future events. This mode of divination ... has been transmitted from age to age in Cornwall; and still exists among the vulgar, who resort to some well of celebrity at particular seasons and there observe the bubbles that rise, and the state of the water, whether troubled or pure, on their throwing in pins or pebbles, and thence read their future destiny.'

The name 'pin wells' or 'pinnal' clearly derives from the offerings made. In many parts of the country there is clear evidence that the pins were bent before being thrown in, although no such pins are known to have been recovered from Leicestershire wells. The practice is known to have continued until at least the nineteenth century in some parts of England and Wales. Most typically the pins were bent in two places; this deliberate damage echoes the similar bending or breaking of swords, knives, coins and other metal items which is familiar from archeological finds of all periods from iron age to medieval periods. Such

2

ritually-damaged goods are usually deposited in water, such as ancient wells, or major rivers such as the Thames, where 'mudlarks' have recovered a wide selection of such items. The best explanation is that an inanimate object was thereby 'killed' and its normal use transferred to spiritual purposes [4].

Wells are sometimes found in, or closely adjacent to, churches. This could be for simple practical needs such as providing the water for baptism, ritual ablutions and cleansing of the vessels used in the Mass. Add to that the fact that early priests lived in their churches and needed water for day-to-day living. A number of wells are in the walls of churchyards. Perhaps wells half-in and half-out churchyards were once thought to be suitable places for early baptism rituals.

But this does not solve the problem of whether the church was built to christianise an already sacred site, or whether a purely practical requirement for water led to a spring acquiring a sacred reputation.

Several wells in the county (Beeby, Burton Lazars, Caldecott, Hinckley, Wymeswold) and nearby Cropwell Bishop (Nottinghamshire), all had the name Stockwell. Rather than assuming this was a place where livestock were watered, sometimes this may originate from Old English *stoc* which can mean 'holy place' (although it more commonly denotes tree stump(s)) [5]. The Beeby Stockwell is still referred to as a holy well and is close to the church. The Wymeswold Stockwell issued from the side of the churchyard mound (but has now been culverted).

Beeby well

An introduction to

Ancient crosses

Although many crosses have been reduced to stumps, or disappeared altogether, Leicestershire is fortunate in having several examples of late Anglo-Saxon crosses , particularly Rothley and Sproxton, and others from the medieval period onwards. In all parts of the county the erection of crosses continues unabated and many twentieth century crosses and village war memorials confuse the unwary by imitating earlier styles, or by being heavy-handed 'restorations' of ancient crosses.

All Leicestershire Anglo-Saxon crosses, except one, are from the same type of stone which suggests they were produced at the same place. As with Anglo-Saxon crosses elsewhere in Britain, the sculptors were clearly familiar with styles of decoration used in north-west France.

Crosses are of interest not only in their own right, but because they raise so many questions. Do they represent the first stages of christianisation of a pagan site, perhaps replacing or being carved from an earlier standing stone? Why do so many so-called 'crosses' not have any signs of ever having been so surmounted? Why are the stepped bases often impractically steep with treads so narrow it would be difficult to stand there long, even for preaching purposes? Are the earliest crosses christian at all?

It is difficult to support the pious assumption that every cross must have been erected after the introduction of christianity. Among ancient Egyptians and eastern Buddhists, indeed throughout most of the world, the pre-christian sanctity of the cross is readily apparent. Long before it became the symbol of Christ's passion the cross was a fertility/virility symbol. Indeed at the time of the early Church the cross was so generally recognised as pagan that its use was forbidden by the Church fathers. As with similar examples from throughout the country, the splendid Anglo-Saxon cross surviving at Sproxton is surmounted by the equal-armed wheel cross, which to its carver would have been recognised as a sun-symbol.

Some crosses are close to churches (usually just to the south) and are termed 'preaching crosses'; others are in the centre of towns or villages and are often known as 'market crosses'. There is no clear distinction of purpose - market crosses may well have been preached from; preaching crosses may have been the location of various traders. Although it may surprise us, throughout the medieval period it was commonplace for fairs to take place in churchyards. Certainly

4

crosses became the place where official proclamations were read, where rules for commerce (e.g. weights and measures) were laid down, where oaths were witnessed and sometimes where justice and punishment were dispensed. As an extension of this, the shaft of the cross may have been deliberately used as the shaft (gnomon) of a sundial. The size of the shadow would have also enabled reasonably accurate monitoring of solstices and other elementary calandrical functions.

By their nature, crosses become landmarks and meeting places, but it is unclear if the site of crosses had such a function before the surviving cross was built. No doubt some crosses replace smaller standing stones, timber shafts or venerable trees (direct evidence for this is available in Cornwall with its multitude of medieval wayside crosses) [1]. Such sites would have been associated with the old religions but, however much the Church might oppose their veneration, it could not remove the landmarks which were basic to the lives of the people.

In the post-Freudian twentieth century it is easy to see these monuments as phallic. Indeed the cross at Clackmannan (Scotland) has in close proximity a distinctly phallic stone, and several Cornish stones and Yorkshire 'crosses' survive which are similar anatomical approximations. To this day in India there are many temples whose holy-of-holies is a stone lingam; India and the British Isles are only the two geographical extremes of a once-common culture. It is probable that their creators saw them not as 'sex symbols' but as more complex symbols of fertility standing on the mother earth.

Although the cross has for many centuries been regarded as a ubiquitous symbol for the christian crucifixion, this has not always been the case. Accurate translation of the Greek New Testament reveals that nowhere is the instrument of Jesus's death referred to as a 'cross' - the word used translates as 'tree'. In many ways that makes the symbolism more complex, because it resonates with all the deeply-rooted mythology of 'The Tree of Life', and makes the Biblical tale seem even closer to the pagan sagas of Odin hanging on the world tree - sacrificing himself to himself. On several Anglo-Saxon crosses foliate decoration is used around the top, and medieval crosses may terminate with palmate or fleur-de-lys patterns.

When the Church first began to use the image of the crucifixion it was referred to as a 'rood', for instance in the Old English poem entitled *The Dream of the Rood*, which emphasises Jesus's agony and suffering. But the everyday meaning of the word 'rood' in those days was as a 'pole' or 'rod'.

The wheel-cross which appears on Anglo-Saxon crosses has little or no resemblance to a crucifix. What it does clearly resemble are the sun-wheels of India. We know that the earliest Anglo-Saxon crosses are those in Ireland and, soon after, in Northumbria. These crosses and their decorative motifs appear to be closely related to Syrian and Coptic work of the period and, even if they were not executed by foreigners, they were probably produced under their influence. This accords well with the origins of monasticism in Ireland, which came about as a result of close contact with Middle Eastern religion.

At the time of the Commonwealth the cross was again spurned, being seen as a symbol of Popery, and as many as possible were destroyed. An Ordinance issued in 1644 extended the removal of crosses and images, previously banned from churches, to include those in open places. After the Restoration the various Jacobite rebellions drew their support from the Continent and therefore had a Roman Catholic taint so it was not until the later eighteenth century that crosses began to reappear in carvings and on the communion tables. A study of the carvings on gravestones will confirm that before about 1760 crosses do not appear and only begin as discrete accompaniments to the figure of Faith. Even well into the nineteenth century gravestone carvers were at pains to differentiate between crucifixes and crosses.

Even when they have not been decapitated not all 'crosses' originally had crosses on them. 'Lantern heads', or capitals with niches for statues, or simply octagonal capitals, are also common. In some parts of Britain the terminal is a stone 'fircone' - a symbol of fertility that was subsequently modified into a stylised 'pineapple' and thus ornamented many a pair of grand gateposts. The cross as fertility symbol has been fully discussed by Irwin [2] and Bryce [3]. The old High Cross in Leicester, now in the Marketplace, exhibits another frequent alternative - a ball. Such balls have been seen as suggestive of sun-symbolism and we know that in India the early Sanskrit texts refer to daily sun-worship rites which entail clockwise circumambulation of pillars.

Again, looking to India, we find clear evidence that would account for the universal stepped base. Up to the present day when a holy man dies there he is buried beneath a stepped mound surmounted by a phallic symbol, perpetuating an association between death and procreation. In Egyptian tomb paintings the Stepped Mound does double-duty for the tomb of Osiris and as the throne on which the new king is consecrated. The Primordial Mound was simultaneously tomb and womb. Throughout the world pyramids and ziggurats take a similar form. Even the internal construction of the massive and enigmatic neolithic earthwork of Silbury Hill near Avebury is in the form of steps. Sir Arthur Evans once wrote 'The coincidences of tradition are beyond the scope of accident.'

An introduction to

Standing stones and mark stones

Stones of interest fall into three categories - natural outcrops which have acquired names or legends, surviving standing stones and, lastly, documented standing stones which have now disappeared. Some of these documented stones may have been natural outcrops. Additionally, within Leicestershire there are many small 'mark stones' which have rarely been documented and turn up more or less unexpectedly when exploring. Such stones are small enough to be readily moved from their original location, and it is nearly impossible to establish if they are of any great antiquity.

Stones of moderate size are themselves hardly unusual. But stones erected as landmarks have certain characteristics which strongly suggest their deliberate siting. A few are long in shape and have clearly been intentionally stood upright. Some of these might be stone gateposts but these are inevitably on modern field boundaries and will normally show evidence of attachments for the gate. Quite possibly some stone gateposts are relocated standing stones; but this is difficult to establish and any stone now a gatepost is best disregarded.

Smaller, boulder-shaped stones of interest are typically of a different rock type to those common in the locality. Leicestershire has many varied rocks which can be quarried and even more when glacial erratics are considered. This makes it comparatively easy to use a distinctive stone as a landmark. Such smaller stones often stand near ancient crossroads or are adjacent to the churchyard wall. Some stand quite close to the church itself. Some stones have flattened sides which may accurately align with nearby ancient features, such as the church. Or the shape of the stone may distinctly point north-south or east-west.

Where a stone was not particularly distinctive it may, in earlier times, have been deliberately whitened. In Yorkshire, Cheshire, Derbyshire and Staffordshire there are stones where this custom is continued (e.g. the Broad Stone in Leek, Staffordshire). Early in the nineteenth century it was recorded that tombstones in Glamorganshire were limed three times a year - at Easter, Whitsun and Christmas. No such rituals are known in Leicestershire but a pub in Hinckley used to be known as The White Stone. There is a stone near Mowsley which has a remarkably white natural colour on its top surface.

Where stones are in villages or near roads and junctions it is inevitable that road widening and repairs will require stones to be moved. No doubt many have been entirely lost or used for building foundations. Documentary sources reveal that many well-known stones have gone and we can only speculate how many unremarkable and unrecorded minor stones have disappeared.

Many deeds and similar documents relating to land refer to boundary stones. Across in Cambridgeshire at the boundary between Croyland and Spalding is a stone known as St Guthlac's Cross with a Latin hexameter which, translated, reads: This rock, I say, is Guthlac's utmost bound'. (St Guthlac was the founder of Croyland Abbey.) The custom of beating the bounds at Rogationtide in May appears not to have been maintained in Leicestershire but has been revived in Crich, Derbyshire where the parishioners walk the fourteen mile perimeter, exposing overgrown boundary stones and, not only offering prayers, but also hearing the vicar invoke the ancient threat 'Cursed be he which translateth the bounds of his neighbours.' [1]

The name 'beating of the bounds' refers to the use of willow wands to vigorously strike the boundary stone or marker - and, it seems, until recent times the location of these markers was firmly implanted in the minds of young children by also beating them, or upending them, or otherwise mistreating them - a fate which may also befall a new curate.

The boundaries of ecclesiastical parishes normally have their origins in Anglo-Saxon times, presumably with the formation of nucleated village settlements in the country during the mid-Saxon era. The priests jealously guarded their parish boundaries, as this affected their rights of tithe. But the exact boundaries have often changed and subdivided, perhaps in 1662 (when the parish boundary became a key factor in the management of the Poor Law) and more radically in 1889, when the concept of *civil* as well as ecclesiastical parishes was created. Much local government tinkering and the national changes to country boundaries in 1974 have led to the present parish boundaries being an unreliable indicator of the exact line of ancient limits. The earliest Ordnance Survey maps at 6' scale show parish boundaries before many of these changes, but they can usually only be accessed at county Record Offices [2].

The result of all this means that stones lying between villages *may* have been boundary stones, but often the present-day parish boundaries shown on 1:25,000 Ordnance Survey maps will not confirm this. Only if the boundary still follows a stream, ancient earthwork or other persistent feature can we be confident that it was primarily a boundary marker. But, looking at this from the opposite direction in time, we should not be too confident that the stone was put there to be a marker. If, when someone was looking to set out or change boundaries, it was essential to fit in as many suitable landmarks as possible. There is nothing more logical than to take in an existing substantial boulder and, with no further effort, make it into a mark stone. And does that not also allow the boundary-maker to move, perhaps only a short distance, a stone that had been set up many centuries before, to make it fulfil the function of an accurate landmark?

The status of 'possible' boundary marker can be easily confered on many of the stones described, but rarely can this be confirmed with any confidence. Neither does it give any firm indication of the date when the stone was set up or whether or not it was moved from a nearby location. We must be content to record their present-day existence and accept all the enigmas they present.

Stones in the middle of villages present slightly less ambiguity. According to Sir G.L. Gomme [3], when a village was first established a stone was set up. To this stone the head man of the village made an offering once a year. Among northern people, princes and leaders were commonly elected at assemblies in or around stone circles. Eric, King of Sweden, was so chosen at Uppsala in 1396. In Norway each of the electors sat on a stone during the formal proceedings. Norwegian tradition also associates stone circles with judicial courts. French cromlechs served as open-air tribunals. Slightly closer to home, the hundred court of Stone in Somerset was held early in the morning at a standing stone on a hill. The stone was hollow and the practice was to pour into the cavity a bottle of port wine. We can but guess what ritual libations may have been previously offered.

From early documentary sources it is clear that stones were one of the many natural features where the pre-christian religions had their focus. Unfortunately these documents are all from christian sources. The earliest dates to around 650ce when Eligius, bishop of Noyon, pleaded that no christian should 'place lights at temples, or stones, or springs, or trees, or at sanctuaries, or at places where three ways meet.' [4] Maybe he was drawing biblical precedent from Isaiah (Isaiah 57:6), who has an outburst against stone worshippers. Soon after Eligius' time Bede complains in his work *On auguries* that people are such fools that they will bring offerings to 'earthfast stone or tree or well-spring'.

The Northumbrian priest's law of 1008-1024 specified a penalty 'if there is on anyone's land a sanctuary round a stone or a tree or a spring or any such nonsense'. About the same time Cnut promulgated a law which included: 'It is heathen practice if one worships idols, namely if one worships heathen gods and the sun or the moon, fire or flood, wells of stone or any kind of forest trees, or if one practices witchcraft or encompasses death by any means, either by sacrifice or divination, or takes part in any such delusions.' [5]

However, this Christian contempt for stones does not have biblical support, for Moses commands Israel with the injunction 'If you make me an altar of stone do not make it of dressed stones; for if you use a tool on it, you profane it' (Exodus 20:25). When Joshua builds an altar on Mount Ebal he refers to this injunction (Joshua 8:31). When the Temple was built there was 'neither hammer, nor axe, nor any tool of iron, heard in the house while it was in building' (1 Kings 6:7). Furthermore, Christ is described as 'the stone that the builders rejected' (Luke 20:17).

Why is the veneration of stones so deep-seated? Marie-Louise von Franz, a psychologist who worked extensively with Carl Jung, suggests that the Self, the 'innermost nucleus of the psyche' is 'symbolised with special frequency in the form of a stone, precious or otherwise.' This is 'perhaps because the stone symbolises mere existence at the farthest remove from emotions, feelings, fantasies and discursive thinking. In this sense the stone symbolises what is perhaps the simplest and deepest experience - the experience of something eternal that man can have in those moments when he feels immortal and unalterable.' [6]

Although I know of over forty substantial stones in Leicestershire and Rutland, they have neither the size nor the abundance of some in other parts of the country, such as Cornwall or the Pennine areas. The stones discussed here rarely seem to have the function of mark stones on straight alignments, as described by John Michell [7], but this may be because too many have been destroyed for the pattern to be discernable.

There is no clear evidence to suggest when any of the stones described were placed in their present positions or even that their placement had special significance. Because some standing stones elsewhere in the country are clearly of great antiquity and appear to act as significant landmarks, it is reasonable to suppose that at least some of Leicestershire's examples also have similar origins. It seems worthwhile to give greater prominence to this easily-lost aspect of our heritage, even though it means including stones which, if the truth were known, are 'modern' or 'accidentally' placed.

Much excellent fieldwork on the stones of Leicestershire was carried out in the early 1970s by Paul Devereux and Andrew York [8]. During the years 1987-90 I revisited all the sites described by them together with any others known to me. Nevertheless there are probably many more interesting stones lurking behind hedgerows and the following information should not be regarded as complete or definitive.

None of the stones described are protected as scheduled ancient monuments and all could disappear at any time. Only through people taking an interest in them and visiting them is there any possibility of their long-term survival. My aim is not simply to provide a record but to stimulate readers to visit (with land owners' permission) and, ideally, to discover for themselves more examples.

An introduction to

Medieval church carvings

I have attempted to draw attention to the wide range of figurative carving that forms an unjustly neglected part of our medieval heritage. Above all, I hope it encourages others, especially those not normally interested in the Church and its buildings, to get out and visit such places.

This information does not attempt to be definitive - there are still many churches in Leicestershire and Rutland that I have not visited, or have been unable to get inside. Nor does this book do justice to the many other architectural and ecclesiastical treasures in the county's churches - it is assumed the serious 'church crawler' will have a copy of Pevsner [1] and, perhaps, the NADFAS guide to church furnishings [2].

A pair of binoculars will help greatly when studying many of these carvings.

The large majority of churches in Leicestershire and Rutland date back to medieval times and visible parts frequently date to the thirteenth and early fourteenth centuries. A surprising number of interesting ancient carvings, mostly in stone but sometimes in wood, have survived later attempts at iconoclasm and heavy-handed restoration. The craftsmanship varies from quaint, clearly local efforts to comparatively sophisticated displays of the stonemasons' skills, with faces and creatures in most animated postures.

There is considerable difficulty in closely dating stone carvings. The same type of tools were used over long periods; external carvings which have begun to erode may be re-cut; above all, stylistic variations seem to relate primarily to the individual stone-masons. Changes in fashion in church decoration were probably transmitted by the masons and, in general, it seems that the masons had considerable control over the details of their activities [3]. I have been informed that masons currently working on the restoration of one of our cathedrals have, by tradition, the right to add whatever decorative motifs they choose. Something of this freedom was expressed when the recent reconstruction of the south transept of York Minster incorporated roof bosses designed around themes suggested by a *Blue Peter* competition.

A number of our churches have traces of Anglo-Saxon or Norman carving. The relevant church guide books will proudly boast that the Christian faith has been followed on that site for 800, 900 even 1000 years. But there are also a greater number of churches with carvings of the medieval period which have

11

display motifs which have nothing to do with Christian teachings and everything to do with the old nature gods. Many of these can be tentatively dated to the thirteenth and fourteenth centuries, although similar carvings are clearly the efforts of Victorians to 'restore' or copy these features.

After a few close inspections of such carvings, it will be apparent that human or animals forms may be depicted in a wonderful variety of styles, from the naturalistic to the grotesque. It is strongly suspected this is a continuation of the Celtic head cults, where shrines would be decorated with skulls set in specially constructed niches. Several archaeological excavations have revealed pairs of pillars with suitable facilities. The custom, which was retained until comparatively recently, of placing the heads of executed felons over the gateway entrances to cities had its roots in the same practices.

Although decorative carved heads are frequently stylised and often intriguingly grotesque, there are certain traits which specifically suggest pre-christian ideas. These include depictions of green man and foliate heads, devouring and biting heads, severed and multiple heads, glaring eyes, beaked faces, mermaids and mermen, hermaphrodites, dragons and serpents, dragon-slayers, mallet-wielding figures, lunar and solar heads, faces with protruding tongues and mouth-pulling or 'girning' faces. As the following comments suggest, each of these can be seen as a memory, or perhaps deliberate evocation, of pre-christian deities.

The glib assumption of church historians that pre-Reformation christianity was closely related to post-Victorian versions seems to fit the facts poorly, if at all. This fascinating hiatus is worthy of a book unto itself but for the moment it is best to assume that, at least in the minds of the pre-Reformation common people, there was little difference between christian practices and the 'pagan' ones that had evolved over many millennia before.

To what extent the medieval clergy practised a tangled web of old and new religions is now impossible to unravel, but I suspect that the reality owes little to what most history books try to sell us.

The surviving medieval carvings are often among the best features of the church but the guide books rarely draw attention to them. This is so consistent one begins to suspect a 'conspiracy of silence' among church recorders and historians. Written history is always from the pen of the victors and never more so than when the conflict is over faith and dogma. But the evidence of historical objects can sometimes speak more loudly than what is published. Whether deliberate or not, any historian working only from written sources would entirely miss these impressive and widespread carvings and the story that they continue to tell.

What sort of carvings are so neglected by the churches' historians? Not the splendid Norman tympanums and fonts which depict a soldier-cum-saint figure dispatching one or more draconian beasts. These appear to fit neatly with the idea of St Michael, or another of the host of canonised dragon-slayers, putting paid to the forces of evil. But it is most likely that the carvers of such scenes would know better the Norse tale of Odin slaying the Midgard serpent, or the tales of Celtic heroes such as Beowulf and Llud dispatching local dragons, as have come down to us in the Welsh *Mabinogion* and the Irish Celtic lore.

It is the term 'grotesques' which obliquely alludes to the figures which history disfavours. Grimacing gargoyles around the roof or tower are, according to more than one parish guide, an illustration of how the forces of evil have been banished to the outside of the church. But why do so many naves and even chancel arches also display corbel heads with similar features?

Not only is it surprising that such carvings were being made at least as late as the fourteenth century, but so many have survived various restorations and deliberate and literal ecclesiastical iconoclasm. It raises the question - when did England become christian?

There is evidence to suggest that from the seventh century there was an attempt to forbid worship at sites other than churches. This was a simple law to circumvent - followers of the old faiths simply built images of their gods into the churches. Of unique quality and quantity are the eighth century carvings at Breedon on the Hill. At least one of these shows mixed pagan and christian influences - a fragment of cross shaft which is said to depict Adam and Eve with, in an adjacent panel, the Entry into Valhalla. What is certain is that the Breedon artists were strongly influenced by Coptic art, which fits in well with assumptions about the strong connections established by the Roman Church between the Middle East and all parts of Europe [4]. Similar parallels, this time with Persian art, have been detected for the twelfth century carvings which abound in the crypt of Canterbury cathedral [5].

Yet many carvings with pagan-inspired symbolism appear to date much later - to the thirteenth and fourteenth centuries, which is well after the time the royal court, and therefore the higher nobility, had accepted christianity. But how deep did this acceptance go? As late as the fifteenth century the Divine Right of Kings, a distinctly pre-christian concept, was still being invoked. The Restoration of Charles II in the seventeenth century brought with it a revival of pre-christian customs such as tree veneration - in the form of Royal Oak Day and other Maytime customs which had been deliberately suppressed by the Puritans.

If the nobility of the land still believed in a combination of old and new faiths, we can be sure that the common folk held on to beliefs and lore which had, at best, a superficially Christian appearance.

The pre-Reformation churches abounded with images of gods - old and new together, and probably more of the former until the cult of the crucifixion slowly emerged in later medieval times to dominate all the old rood screens, built to divide the chancel from the nave. It was only in the sixteenth century that the church began to attack the beliefs of the common people. Witch trials have been a subject of fascination to many people. The trial records make it clear that quite often the leader of the witches' celebrations was the local priest, which suggests that the clergy of the sixteenth century were willing to support the spiritual requirements of their parishioners in a more enlightened manner than the dogma of the One True Way should allow [6]. This indication of the rift between the senior, witch-hunting clergy and the 'grassroots' priests more than allows an explanation for at least the survival, if not the creation, of images of the old gods within the churches.

Slim though the evidence is it seems that veneration for these old gods had remained more or less close to the surface of church worship. Consciously or otherwise the incumbent allowed the old beliefs of his congregation to be more or less explicitly sustained.

In spite of all the efforts during and after the Reformation to rid the Church of its all-too-visible pre-christian roots, the current Anglican liturgy is still a rich source of survivals of the old faiths. Perhaps the clearest instance is the rite of infant baptism - petitionary prayers that but for a word or three would be spells supported by the sacred names of the old gods, with the timeless use of water and a candle that owes nothing to Biblical precedent and everything to what the self-same vicar might slander as 'Devil Worship'.

History as the Church would want us to know it is that the missionaries came to Dark Age Britain and an entirely novel religion took root and rapidly flourished with the prompt demise of any old faiths. History, as read between the lines and by what physically survives, is that the missionaries came and adapted the sites, the festivals and the rites of the deeply-rooted old faiths as little as possible. The new god's annual resurrection was a familiar concept. That He died to redeem everyone from sin and evil was a new idea, not least because the ideas of sin and evil were a bit too abstract compared to the more direct and tangible roles of Anglo-Saxon and Scandinavian deities and their wonderful tales that made such excellent fireside entertainment.

Moving back from such speculative thoughts to the physical aspects of the surviving carvings, it is worth noting that one of the worst sins of the Victorian 'restorers' was to remove from sculpture all traces of medieval paint. The evidence of the restorers themselves and coloured prints of the pre-Victorian era show that no medieval carving was complete without a good deal of colour. Indeed, it appears that nearly as much money was spent on the painting and gilding of a sculpture as on its carving [7]. To imagine these old carvings in their original form we need to try to see them not as bare stone but as painted, often in what would now seem garish colour combinations. The backgrounds and faces might be orange ochre with costumes in green highlighted with red ochre.

14

Blue appears to have been less frequently used, perhaps because non-fading pigments were expensive. One of the few churches in Leicestershire where the original colours can be viewed is Ashby Folville. A number of others, notably Lutterworth, have restored roof bosses to some semblance of their original splendour.

Anglo-Saxon and Norman carvings in Leicestershire and Rutland

Anglo-Saxon carvings.

The Anglo-Saxon crosses have been discussed above. Of the other carvings of this period without doubt the surviving sculptures at Breedon on the Hill are one of the county's greatest treasures. A set of four tombstones from Thurnby (now in the Jewry Wall Museum) are also dated as late Anglo-Saxon, presumably of the early christian period, but there is only one similar set in Britain.

Norman carvings

With the Norman Conquest there is simultaneously a period of extensive church building and rebuilding and the frequent use of carved stone. As with other parts of the country there are many survivals of this activity, with some very fine figurative carving.

In the county there are fine examples of Norman tympanum at Hallaton, Stoney Stanton (both depicting dragons and their protagonists), Essendine, Greetham, Little Casterton and Ridlington. Not all these occupy their original position - for instance, the Hallaton one is in the wall of the porch.

Norman arches and doorways frequently survive, although normally only decorated with the characteristic dogs-tooth ornament. Also plentiful are Norman fonts, although many are plain or decorated with architectural arcading (which supposed to suggest the baptised person entering the Temple of God).

Other examples of figurative Norman carving include a figure holding what appears to be a large hammer which is now situated in a passageway to the vestry inside Church Langton church. Although not a sophisticated piece of carving it does evoke a feeling of power. It appears to be a representation of the mallet-wielding Scandinavian deity usually known as Thor and is usually dated to the Norman period.

Medieval figurative carvings

Figurative medieval carvings predominantly depict subjects and themes which owe little, if anything, to Biblical precedents, and can be much more easily attributed to a continuation of pre-christian beliefs [8]. The following is merely a brief guide.

Green men and foliate heads

The most easily recognised pagan influence would seem to be where a man's head is not only surrounded by foliage but has branches sprouting from the mouth or nose. Such carvings are known to date back to Roman times. There is a strong popular tradition that these were carved to depict the Old God of fertility and rebirth who surfaces in folklore under various names - Herne the Hunter, Robin Goodfellow, Robin Hood and so on. Academic scholarship has rejected this claim, preferring instead to argue that their carvers saw them as images of Lust or other Deadly Sins [9].

Hallaton Green Man

Whatever the original truth they are invariably forceful images and, to the modern mind at least, have profoundly pagan associations. The Green Man motif is perhaps one of the most evocative of all the carved images we encounter in churches. A TV programme and two books have been published devoted just to this theme [10].

Horned and big-eared heads

Another form of these old gods was the Horned One, often known as Cunnunos or Herne the Hunter. So far I have not discovered any stag-antlered heads in the county but there are several with short, cow-like horns. Many more look similar at first glance, but turn out to be faces with long ears. It may be that faces with hare-like ears should be seen as a bowdlerised version of the same (perhaps even being a result of re-carving by christian vandals).

'Girning' or face-pulling heads

Among the most hideous faces are those which are, literally, pulling faces - with both hands, or occasionally only one, stretching the mouth. In the north-west of England, until comparatively

Thorpe Arnold girning face

recently, face-pulling or 'girning' championships were held where the contestants put their heads through a horse collar and pull the most frightening faces possible [11]. 'Girning' gargoyles - human and bestial - frequently repose around the roofs of our churches. There are also several excellent examples on the corbels within the nave of other churches.

One church guide describes such a figure as 'a man with toothache'. But a less fanciful interpretation is that these faces appear to be a polite version of the Sheela-na-gig carvings, otherwise known as female exhibitionists, who evoke images of their fecundity by using their hands in a similar way to prominently display other parts of their anatomy.

Tongue-pokers

It would be too much to expect the survival in a church of any carving whose masculinity was too obvious - although there is a clearly male exhibitionist in Queniborough church roof. But, just as the girning faces may be a polite version of female exhibitionists, so tongue-poking faces have been seen as the counterpart for the male [12].

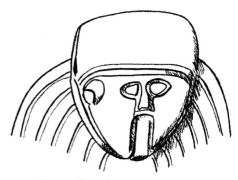

Above: *Greetham tongue-poker*
Below: *Beaked head on Norman doorway at St Mary in Arden, Market Harborough*

Beaked heads

This is a striking but rather obscure motif, usually associated with Norman arches. There is perhaps some subtle continuity with those winged, beaked horses which feature in Celtic art or with aspects of Odin-worship where bird-costumes and masks were essential to the more shamanistic aspects, such as journeying to the Otherworlds.

One of the best local examples of beak heads is at Tickencote. Others can be seen at Cold Overton and the ruined St Mary in Arden church at Market Harborough.

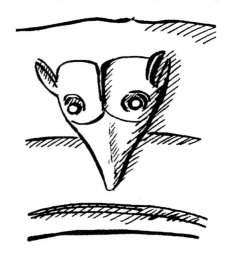

Dragons and dragon-slayers

Although all the motifs listed in previous sections can be interpreted as being pre-christian the history of their symbolism is often difficult to establish. It is with dragon-slayers we have our clearest view of the deliberate re-use of existing mythology by the early English Church.

As is well known, throughout Britain there are many fine depictions of fearsome mythical beasts being impaled by more-or-less saintly figures. For convenience I will refer to the victims as dragons, although serpents - winged or otherwise - and griffins or wyverns seem to be used as almost interchangeable names.

Otherwise quite modest parish churches may contain dragon-slaying sculptures of great artistic and historical interest. Often such carvings are from the Norman period although the subject has always remained popular - the massive post-war bronze sculpture on the new Coventry Cathedral is especially well-known.

Fairly predictably the Church claims such scenarios as showing the triumph of their 'One True Way' over the forces of 'evil' and, more often than not, the church guide-book will name the human protagonist as St Michael. In some cases the church may be dedicated to him, but not necessarily. As an extension of this approach dedications to St Michael and All Angels have been said to imply that the Church had to pull all the stops out to conquer the local pagans!

But a moment's pause for mental breath will allow a flood of questions to surface. Who started the claim that the dragons depicted the 'forces of evil' (i.e. paganism)? Why should the figure be St Michael, when a wide range of other dragon-defying heroes are known? Why are some figures depicted as carrying swords or spears instead of croziers, but are all referred to as saints and not bishops or soldiers? Why do these carvings often depict secondary human or animal figures, and what do they signify? I regret that it is beyond the scope of this publication to answer all these questions, which I have approached elsewhere [13].

Suffice to say that the carvers saw them less as a permanent conquest of Good over Evil but rather as a Tao-like duality where the strength of the Light can only be seen when surrounded by Darkness. Indeed, the Norman carvings show just this - a frozen combat in which there is no victor; the combatants will remain in contention until the end of time, or at least until the processes of erosion are completed. Only at a later date do artists depict the saint in a victorious pose over a defunct demon.

Apart from the saints commonly associated with dragons this hagiographical attribute extends to several lesser figures. In Rutland there are two churches dedicated to St Guthlac, at Stathern and Branston. In the east window of

Thorpe Arnold font

Stathern church one of the four figures portrayed in the eighteenth century stained glass is St Guthlac, standing on a lurid red dragon. The church guide states 'He was a Saxon nobleman, who had lived a wild and reckless life, but after his conversion he went to live as a hermit in the fen land around Crowland in Lincolnshire.' These events date to the end of the seventh century, according to a chronicler writing a few decades later. Guthlac's greater claim to fame was to be involved in the founding of the Abbey at Croyland which was then dedicated to him, and a lost sculpture on the west front showed him surmounting a demonic creature. Another stained glass image of St Guthlac is in Eaton church, where he is also shown in a similar pose.

The folklore of the county has little to offer in the way of dragon legends apart from the tale of a griffin taking over the well at Griffydam, which is probably spurious .

There are some records of the medieval gilds in Leicester performing an annual procession called 'Riding the George' which included elaborate costumes for George, his horse and the dragon. Although this event seems to have stopped by the 1560s, to this day the Leicester gilds hold St George in high esteem - there is a nineteenth century sculpture of him in their 'shrine' at St Mary de Castro.

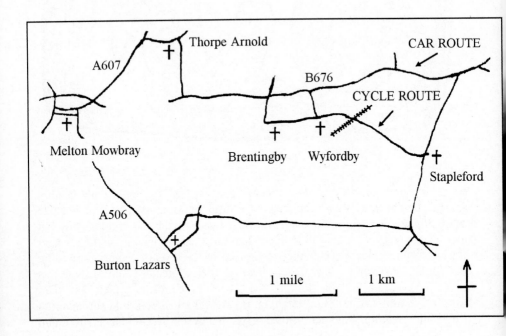

Tour 1 - starts Melton Mowbray

Part 2

Tour 1 Melton Mowbray

A short tour for starters

OS Sheets 129 and 130
Approximately ten miles

MELTON MOWBRAY

We start in the town for convenience. The church of St Mary (129:753191) hardly ranks as 'little-known Leicestershire' as it is among the largest and most beautiful parish churches in England and well-worth investigation. Among the many splendours there are a number of royal coats of arms - pride of place is understandably given to those of Charles I which hang above the transcept arch in the nave. There are several effigies. The knight in the nave has an unusually detailed rendition of the coat of mail - look too for the peculiar shape on his left which is intended to be a crushed frog and was originally underneath the point of his (now-missing) sword.

The town once had at least six crosses:
- Kettleby Cross, which stood outside the town to the south of the present A607 (O.S. Grid Ref. approx.747198)
- Sheep Cross which stood towards the north of Nottingham Street (near where the offices of the Melton Times now stand);
- Corn Cross which stood at the south of Nottingham Street (near where Dixons now are);
- Butter Cross or High Cross which stood near the centre of the market place (in 1986 this was recreated and now stands in approximately the original position);
- Sage Cross which stood at the east of Sherrard Street roughly where the stalls of the Tuesday market stop today;
- Thorpe Cross which stood to the east of the town near where the B676 meets the A607 (O.S. Grid Ref. 757193).

The modern version of the Butter Cross has recently been carved and placed in the Market Place. If one does chose to stop and investigate, then look across to the buildings of W.H. Smith and the card shop (previously Samuel's jewellers) opposite. These appear to occupy the site of the gateway of the Norman castle - the basements contain substantial masonry. What is now King Street would have been the entrance to the castle, which presumably stood to the north.

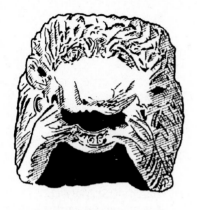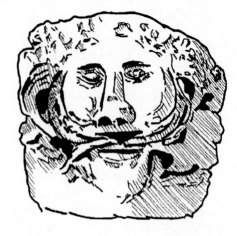

Thorpe Arnold corbels

Follow signs for Grantham onto the A607. Past Tesco's supermarket and up the hill is:

THORPE ARNOLD

In the midst of this predominantly-Georgian village is the church of St Mary (129:770201). Much of the structure is from the thirteenth century, but the font is Norman. It depicts five dragons attacking a sword-wielding, shield-bearing man (see illustration on page 19).

Near the font is a decorated capital with two sun-burst faces. Although these may also be Norman, Pevsner prefers to persuade us that they are fourteenth or early fifteenth century.

Most impressive are the vigorous carvings in the nave which once supported the roof timbers. They include a Green Man, a cow, a girning animal, and a curious figure which is best considered as a contortionist with his head between his legs - although this interpretation would make him a male exhibitionist of megaphallic proportions. I strongly suspect that these carvings are thirteenth century in date. They are among the best carvings of their kind in the county and no one passing through Thorpe Arnold should miss them. The key for the church can be obtained from the white-painted cottage to the east of the churchyard.

My only regret is that in the last few years ugly heaters have been insensitively put up by these corbels. It would seem that the local population hold these splendid sculptures in contempt, as the church guide - at 52 A4-sized pages one of the most impressive for any Leicestershire church - makes no reference to any of them; except for a fuzzy photograph of the font.

To the west of the tower is the base of a medieval cross. To the south-west of the village are enigmatic earthworks along the steep slope of the hill. These have never been conclusively dated but are presumed to be medieval in date.

Take the track from the south of the church and turn left at the B676. First right (at a crossroads near the brow of a small hill) will take you through:

BRENTINGBY

The cute little steeple of the church comes into view - but be prepared for a surprise when you see the rest of the building. This is definitely a redundant church with a difference! Look out for the seventeenth century farmhouse near church. The village names means the settlement of a person known as Brentings. Interestingly, such a person is mentioned in the Old English epic poem *Beowulf.*

Car drivers may wish to turn back now to the B676, as the level crossing at Wyfordby is normally locked (cyclists can use the unlocked pedestrian gate).

Just along the road is:

WYFORDBY

This place-name again has an interesting origin - 'the pagan shrine by the ford'. The road over the level crossing takes you eastwards; the course of this road is roughly that of an ancient salt traders' track which would end at the salt pans of the fenlands. (A possible clue to its later status can be noted with the name of the farm at 130:823167 - 'Holygate Farm'; 'gate' is Scandinavian dialect for 'road'.)

Cyclists should continue along the lane to the T-junction and cross straight over, through the gates of Stapleford Park hotel.

Car drivers need to turn right then slow down in the small settlement of Stapleford, turning left into the gates of Stapleford Park hotel.

STAPLEFORD

This little settlement is referred to by locals as 'staplfud' and takes its name from 'the ford marked by post' (from Old English *stapol* meaning 'post').

In the grounds of the prestigious Stapleford Park hotel is St Mary Magdalene church (129:812182) which is in the Gothick style of 1783 with all its original furnishings. The box pews are set college-wise, there is a three-sided communion rail and table, plus a two-decker pulpit, reredos and west gallery. There are various high-quality marble effigies in a variety of ostentatious styles.

The key can be obtained from the hotel reception desk. The seventeenth century hall buildings (now the hotel) have much of interest and are well worth the slight detour.

Roman and Anglo-Saxon remains have been reported in the vicinity. The earthworks of a deserted medieval village can be seen in the fields nearby. Among the more modest buildings are some fine thatched cottages.

Return around the one-way system to the church.

[Those who want to mix and match their versions of my tours should note that Stapleford is close to some sites in Tour Ten.]

Turn left at the entrance gates and take the first right towards:
BURTON LAZARS
Take the first left at the edge of the village (Hollow Lane).

Like all place-names with the element 'Burton', this is an Anglo-Saxon 'burgh town', probably built to defend important settlements from early Viking incursions. In this case the 'important place' was clearly Melton Mowbray - indirect evidence for early prominence of this town.

Burton acquired prominence in its own right in the medieval period, when it was the most important Augustinian leper (hence 'lazar') hospital in England, founded by Roger de Mowbray in the thirteenth century. Although nothing can now be seen apart from humps and hollows the hospital was well-known for its healing spring.

Hollow Lane leads into New Road. Look out for number 27 New Road. In the front garden is a well-maintained pond. The name of the house, however, gives away the significance of this source of water - the Stockwell.

Turn right, with care, at the main road. Car drivers should take the immediate right and pull up near the church.

St James' church is more interesting than first impressions would credit. There is no tower, simply a bell turret. The rather small bells are known locally as the 'ting tangs'. Perhaps the most striking feature is in the churchyard by the roadside - the totally over-the-top monument to William Squire (died 1772). Rococo imagery spills over, such as skulls, serpents and eagles plus the figures of Time, Faith, Hope and Charity. So much of his estate was used to pay for the monument that none was left to meet his other legacies.

Charity appears again in an unusual Swithland slate gravestone to Mary Blower (died 1781). While you are looking for this also keep an eye open for another interesting slate with sheep shears and crook.

Once inside the church, look for the ten musicians carved in wood, supported by grotesque corbels. There are heads carved on the Norman capitals with stiff-leaf decoration above them rather like head dresses. The font is late fourteenth century. All the carvings are well-preserved.

The A606 heads north-west directly into Melton Mowbray.

Tour 2 Wreake valley

A Danish assortment

OS Sheets 129 and 130
Approximately 24 miles

MELTON MOWBRAY
See Tour 1.
Take the A607 towards Leicester and:
KIRBY BELLARS
Coming into the village, right by the road is a prominent mound surmounted by a Scots Pine tree (129:720174). While those familiar with, say, the Wessex landscape would be forgiven for thinking this to be a prehistoric barrow it is actually an eighteenth century prospect mound, intended to allow good views of the formal gardens which once lay towards the now-gone hall.

Just after the petrol station turn right and follow to the end of the quiet cul-de-sac to St Peter's church with its beautiful spire. A small piece of late ninth century Anglo- Saxon frieze was found in the wall of a house (now in the possession of Leicestershire Museums) which gives clear confirmation for the early foundation for the eponymous 'kirk'. Grave-digging in the churchyard revealed evidence for both Roman and Anglo-Saxon occupation.

From 1359 this was the site of an Augustinian monastery and the stump of an ancient cross in churchyard may just possibly date to that period.
Return to the A607 and turn right towards Leicester. Take the next right towards:
ASFORDBY
The three-arch bridge over the Wreake is worth stopping to see (be careful - there are few suitable places to park a car near the bends). Ignoring the modern superstructure, one will quickly notice that the base of the piers are built on medieval cutwaters. There is also an impressive view towards the church and Georgian rectory.
Turn right in the village and right again opposite the garage into All Saint's Close.
At the 'dead' end of Church Lane, by the main road, is a large cross shaft. The base is original although the shaft was replaced in the 1920s after the original was broken in an early motoring accident.

Fragments of an even more interesting cross shaft can be seen in the south aisle of All Saint's church (129:708190). These are from an Anglo-Saxon cross

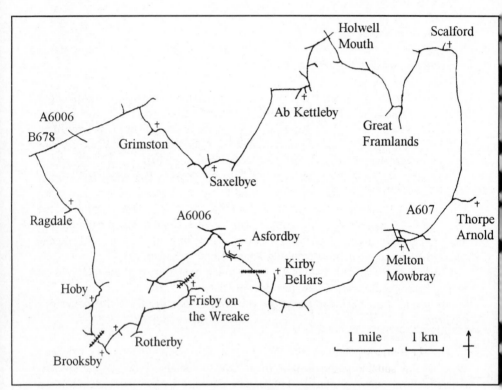

Tour 2 - starts Melton Mowbray

and depict a bishop with crozier, a friendly-looking dragon and interlace decoration. The nave roof held up by twelve musical angels and there are a number of interesting corbel heads in the nave including a girning man. An excellent Green Man is depicted on a nave roof boss. Try to spot the mini girning face on a capital in the south transcept.

To the south of the churchyard is the Georgian rectory which is reputedly haunted, as is a cottage in the nearby street.

Return along Main Street, heading west, and turn left just after the speed de-restriction signs but before the T-junction with the modern bypass. Aim towards Hoby but turn left after about one mile to:

FRISBY ON THE WREAKE

Turn right at the give way signs and pull up.

You will have already noticed the ancient pilgrim cross. This originally stood in the middle of the road junction - an easily-missed cross of five granite setts in the tarmac reveals where it formerly stood (129:694176).

To my knowledge this is the only ancient cross known locally as a 'pilgrim cross' and I suspect that this came from the unusual dedication of the church to St Thomas of Canterbury, that is, Thomas à Beckett. There is no direct evidence of pilgrimages to Frisby, but St Thomas's shrine at Canterbury was the major focus of medieval English pilgrimage, as Chaucer's tales portray. I can only presume that

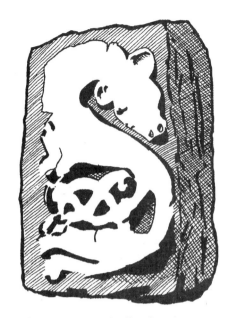

Above: *Asfordby dragon*
Below: *Frisby cross*

27

before the Reformation the church possessed relics of this most highly regarded saint, thereby attracting numbers of local pilgrims. The tower has Norman foundations and there are some carved corbels - including what appears to be a duck.

Although not on the route which I describe, the stump of another cross stands on the A607 Melton to Leicester road where a footpath crosses (129:696171 - it is illegal to park on the verges and great care must be taken as the traffic on this stretch of road is both frequent and fast). The Melton road originally ran through Frisby and the road which now forms the A607 was only created in 1810. Did this cross exist before the road, or is it a simply a large milestone which has become known as a cross?

Ignoring this cross shaft because of the difficulties of access, leave the pilgrim cross and church at Frisby by way of the lane leading south-west. Take the second right to:

ROTHERBY

This quiet village has a small nature reserve, based around a pond, on the left hand side of the street coming into the village. In the village itself is All Saint's church (675166) which is mostly thirteenth and fourteenth century, although there are traces of twelfth century Norman masonry.

Continue through Rotherby and over the cattle grid. At the end turn left and immediate right into the entrance to the college at:

BROOKSBY

The small church of St Michael (671160) has a fourteenth century tower. The still-impressive hall was originally Tudor and the estate has been associated with such people as George Villiers, later Duke of Buckingham, (who ran England for James I) and Lord Cardigan (leader of the Charge of the Light Brigade).

It is also associated with more paranormal events. It is said that shortly before Christmas a ghostly coach and horses rushes towards the hall at midnight. It stops long e ough to unload a weighty item, then dashes off. On other occasions the ghost of a woman may be seen, identified as a former mistress of the house, Lady Caroline. Perhaps it is her skeleton which was discovered by workmen near the Hall in 1891?

One of Leicestershire's most mysterious intrigues was enacted at Brooksby, when George Villiers was still living here after being made Duke of Buckingham. One of his elderly servants, a man named Parker, was visited by the ghost of Villiers' father. The ghost asked Parker to tell his son, the Duke, that he should avoid the company of a specific person if he was to avoid death and destruction. Parker did not expect the imperious Duke to heed such a warning and ignored the ghost's request. Again the ghost appeared and repeated his request more fervently, this time providing Parker with an unspecified secret which would endorse the advice.

Parker went to the Duke who was, as expected, sceptical, although amazed at the secret. The ghost reappeared to Parker to thank him and also to give him a dagger and to tell Buckingham that by such means he would meet his death if he failed to heed the warning. He also informed Parker that he too would die soon after the Duke.

Regardless of this new declaration, Buckingham did not avoid the specified individual. Six weeks later, while visiting Portsmouth, a naval lieutenant named John Fenton (who had sailed under Buckingham's disastrous command) stabbed the Duke to death. And the aged Parker soon followed his master.

Leave the college entrance and turn left; after the bridge keep to the right, heading towards:

HOBY

Turn right in the village and notice the interesting group of buildings on your left, just before the church.

Pronounced 'hoe-by', this attractive village was rebuilt as a 'model' village before the First World War by the Hardcastle family - although the main street still twists and turns.

In the churchyard is the remains of an ancient cross shaft. Part is now the base for a sundial, and the remainder lays against the fence.

Outside the old forge building is a large boulder which has been dubbed the 'Buttock Stone' by one visitor, an epithet which fits remarkably well. It is of a type of rock known to geologists as conglomerate but colloquially as 'puddingstone' or 'breeding stone'. It does have a passing resemblance to a pudding stuffed with currants; 'breeding stone' refers to a long-held folk belief that stones grow in the earth. There is no local outcrop of conglomerate and this boulder must either have been a glacial erratic or deliberately brought some distance.

If in need of good beer and excellent food, the Blue Bell is well worth investigating.

The late-eighteenth century antiquarian Nichols refers to a mound in a meadow near the river which was known as Robin Hood's Barn, but nothing else is known of this.

Twist and turn through the village and, on the outskirts where the road continues to the right, take the lane on the left leading straight on. This agreeably undulating route takes you into:

RAGDALE

To the north of the village is the church of All Saints. Access to this is along a footpath through the field. Where the footpath meets the road is a substantial boulder - probably used as a mounting block.

There is an excellent old cross in the churchyard (129:662199).

Continue north up the hill and turn right onto the B676. This straight stretch of road has its origins in a prehistoric trackway and minor Roman road.

Cross the A6006.
The early origins of this route become clearer here with the impressive views on the left over the Trent valley. The road is following the scarp of a ridge of ironstone; the remains of nineteenth and twentieth century ironstone mines will be encountered shortly but the deposits are known to have been worked since Roman times.

Ragdale (from Nichols)

Take first right to:
GRIMSTON

Stop by the village green and look underneath the chestnut tree where there is an old set of stocks with a large upright boulder nearby (129:564218). While it is tempting to see this as 'Grimr's stone' (Grimr being a nickname of Odin or Woden) we must respect the place-name experts' opinion that the village is the *tun* ('town' i.e. settlement) of a human person called Grimr.

Grimston girning gargoyle

There are accounts of another stone about five feet high which stood in a field near the village (at approx. 686212) but this is known to have been dumped into a pond. Intriguingly, local lore said it 'fell off a star'. While improbable for such a massive rock, meteoric origins for standing stones are a surprisingly common claim in folklore.

The church of St John the Evangelist sits atop a high mound, with the remains of a cross base to the south, on the brink of a high retaining wall. The timber roof bosses inside include a tongue-poker with a crown (or is it

30

Grimston stocks and stone

tufted hair?) and the gargoyles on the tower are most singular. One is girning, another looks like a toothed fish or crocodile, the third is a figure bearing a shield and the fourth is too weathered to identify. There are a number of interesting old slates in the graveyard.

Continue past the church along the road running to the south-west and turn left under the railway bridge into:

Belvoir angel
By kind permission of
Isobel Foster.

31

SAXELBYE

Turn right into Church Lane; car drivers should park at the end of the cul-de-sac.

The church of St Peter (129:700210) has four gargoyles around tower. The south-west one is sitting cross-legged with the lead spout coming out of the rear of his backside - or is it really his front? Four figures on the east window of the chancel have their shoulders above their heads and hands hanging down. Perhaps most special carvings are several small early eighteenth century Swithland slate tombstones with Belvoir angels.

Return along Church Lane and turn right at the give way, taking the lane which heads east

At the three-lanes end by Glebe Farm can be seen a substantial boulder on the verge. Until recently this rather three-sided stone was in the field opposite, but moved when the field changed from pasture to arable.

Turn left and, after about a mile and a half, turn right at the give way to:
AB KETTLEBY

Turn right down Church Lane (unfortunately this is a 'blind' right turn and the street name sign is not visible until after you have turned; if you get to the old re telephone box then you have just missed the turn!).

Pull up in the picturesque setting near the village pond amidst the orange-coloured ironstone cottages. To the side, by a footpath sign, is a small structure which is the holy well (129:724230).

The present well structure is a truncated pyramid just over a yard high and surmounted by what at first glance appears to be an upturned font but was probably a previous basin for the well. This is probably the most attractively situated of the few surviving Leicestershire holy wells and deserves greater prominence. It used to provide a good supply of water until some modern houses were built nearby in the late 1980s. Rheumatic illnesses are said to have been cured by it. Interestingly, the water does not feed into the adjacent pond, but is culverted towards the south, where it presumably once fed the moat to the west of the church of St James the Greater.

Repairs to the floor of the church last century revealed the remains of a Roman tessellated pavement, suggesting that this is another example of a church first built from the ruins of a villa. There is a scratch dial and a Norman font. The pews are original and there are carved bench ends from the late fifteenth century. The church is mostly thirteenth century but 'severely resto ed' in the words of Pevsner.

Before the First World War the plough boys dressed up for est vities on Plough Monday (the first Monday after the 6th January or Twelfth Day). A door-to-door collection was made for food and drink, and the boys' disguises ensured they could exact reprisals against the more tightfisted without fear of retribution. Ab Kettleby was no exception to this custom and indeed the words of their song have been recorded:

Kind master and kind mistresses as you sit around your fire,
To think of us poor ploughboys who plough through mud and mire.
The mud is so very deep and the water runs so clear,
We thank you for your Christmas box and a pitcher of your best beer.
[Sung to the tune of 'Jim the Carter's Lad'.]

Turn back to the main street and turn right to leave the village to the east. Turn left at the A606 then right soon after the Sugar Loaf pub. This will take you to a three-lanes end at the bottom of a hill. In the wood to the north-west is:

HOLWELL MOUTH

The name derives from 'well in a hollow', and the 'hollow' is pronounced (129:727243). Clearly a chalybeate spring, the water course is stained rust brown; this water was also considered to be rather sulphurous tasting. It enjoyed a reputation during the seventeenth and eighteenth centuries as a medicinal spring when there was a stone surround and seats for the invalids who visited it. Although the site is now neglected and overgrown, the water is still flowing and is the source of the River Smite.

Note that this site is not on the nearby footpath and the landowner does not welcome visitors to the spring.

Continue north-east then turn right at the crossroads to the village of Holwell itself.

The thirteenth century church is small and has no dedication. The inside has never been altered in 650 years and there is ancient glass in the east window.

Continue along the village street and leave by the lane leading south-east.

This takes you through the greatly disturbed landscape of the old ironstone mines which operated in the late nineteenth and early twentieth century. One (Brown's Hill Quarry) is now a nature reserve. The ironstone exposures are rich in fossils, although the impressive 'sea floor' of belemnites (fossilised cuttlefish) has been vandalised. Bivalve shellfish fossils can be found in the old quarry faces although bear in mind that removing them is illegal. The mine entrances are gated and within are important winter homes for colonies of bats.

At the three lanes-end at 129:747226 is:

GREAT FRAMLANDS WOOD

The local administrative Hundred of Framland met here at this hill-top site with impressive views of the surrounding countryside. The nearby north-south road is an ancient trackway which originates at Burrough Hill hill fort, to the south of Melton.

Framland derives from the Old English for Fraena's Grove - Fraena may be another spelling of the Anglo-Saxon goddess Freya, who also gives us Friday.

At this three-lanes-end take the left turn and turn left soon after to take the road leading north to:

SCALFORD

The local pronunciation is 'scor'fud'.

Turn first right in the village and pull up by the church (129:763242). It is the only one dedicated to St Egelwin, was a seventh century martyr. Although only recently recognised, there is an Anglo-Viking carving by the rood loft stairs (almost behind the pulpit). The foliate roof bosses and decorative heads are of especial interest; in the roof of the porch is a boss depicting a tongue-poking Green Man. Other carvings of interest include thirteenth century carved heads in the chancel arch capitals and girning gargoyles on the tower.

In the churchyard is the base of a circular medieval cross.

Continue along Church Street and turn right at the give way (taking car of the blind approach from the right). From the village take the road which heads due south towards Melton Mowbray and turn right at the A607

This is near the start of Tour 1. If you have not already investigated Thorpe Arnold church, then bear left at the main road and continue up the hill where the church is easily visible, as this is one aspect of little-known Leicestershire that should not be missed.

Tour 3 Vale of Belvoir

Carvings of all kinds

OS Sheets 129 and 130
Approximately 46 miles

Cyclists should note that, although longer than other tours, the route (with the exception of the part from Harston to Croxton Kerrial) is comparatively flat so, if there is no strong wind, should not prove too strenuous.

Although it would be too much to identify individually the many examples, there is a feast of vernacular architecture in the villages visited. A mixture of ironstone and brick construction (sometimes mixed in the same building) is prevalent, with plenty of traditional pantiles.

WALTHAM ON THE WOLDS

This village straddles the A607 from Melton Mowbray to Grantham. The Royal Horseshoes competes with the Marquis of Granby with both offering old world comfort and hospitality.

At the village crossroads (130:803251) is a circular stone structure with a wooden framework surmounting it which is capped with a conical roof. Although filled in many years ago this structure is recent as it replaced one damaged in stormy weather. It is one of five wells in the village constructed in the Victorian era by the owner of the village, one of the Dukes of Rutland.

In the wall of the churchyard can be seen an iron gate which lets into a small circular stone chamber with a floor one yard below the road level. In this floor, which is about two yards across, is a well in which can be seen water. This is fed by a spring which rose a few yards to one side, for in Victorian times there were houses here and the spring was in the house next to the well it fed, again provided by the Duke of Rutland as a drinking fountain. The spring once flooded across the road but the local council piped it under the road about 1900. It went into disuse after a family living in one of the houses was struck down by diphtheria and buried in the churchyard behind. There are other wells in the village which might tap their water from the same source. One had a hand pump under an elaborate wooden cover some 150 yards away, which can still be seen, though the cover is modern and replaces the original which was damaged in a storm.

The church mostly dates back to about 1300, with two Norman doorways surviving from an earlier structure. The font is also Norman although the Latin

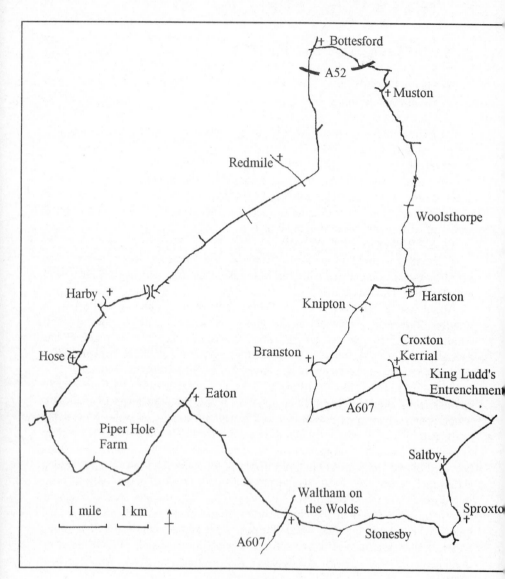

Tour 3 - starts Waltham on the Wolds

> **Cresswell Spring**
>
> Just outside Waltham on the Wolds was Cresswell Spring
> (129:797262). A water authority pumping station was erected near the
> spring and tapped its water for use in Waltham. However, the station is
> now disused and the building in a state of disrepair. The spring site is
> adjacent to the station and covered with a concrete top which has locked
> metal doors. Overflow water from the spring emerges some yards away
> in a hollow and runs away into a nearby stream.
>
> The local legend concerning this holy and healing spring was written
> down by an elderly resident of Waltham, the late George Chester, some
> time in the 1930s. He states the earliest name for the well was the
> Scaldes Well, which he thought had druidical associations. However,
> legend had it that Christ visited Britain and when the pagans were
> converted locally they changed the name of their sacred well to Christ's
> Well, which with the passage of time became known as Cresswell.
>
> The water is said to be very cold and there is the tale of a woman
> who was working in the field near it one hot day when she drank some
> of its water. This, according to Mr Chester's manuscript, 'set the fat
> around her heart' and before the day was out she died. An odd tale for a
> healing spring! The spring is said never to have dried up, even during
> the great drought of 1935.

cross on an almond-shaped halo is probably not original. The oldest survivals are
the Anglo-Saxon coffin lids.

*At the crossroads by the Horseshoes (130:803251), take the minor road
heading north-west (Goadby Road). Continue to the give way signs at the
cross roads and turn right into:*

EASTWELL

The small church of St Michael and All Angels (129:775285) is attractive
from the outside and even more outstanding internally. It is mostly thirteenth
century with a very rare stone chancel screen, dating to the fourteenth century. In
the medieval church the chancel was visually blocked from the nave, as is the
case in eastern Orthodox christianity to this day.

Also from the fourteenth century are some fragments of stained glass showing
a golden-haired angel. Over the south door inside the porch is a Green Man and
a Norman tympanum on the outside.

On the outside of the tower are three gargoyles: one is girning; another is a
horse or dragon head on its side.

Return to the crossroads and continue straight over.

This long, fairly straight road is an ancient salt way and later Roman road.
After about a mile on the right is Piper Hole Farm, which takes its name from

the legend of a piper's hole which is identified with a well on the scarp slope of the Harby Hills. Such legends are known throughout England - there is another recorded for Leicestershire at Shepshed, in a wood which is now cut by the M1. Although there are no details for these Leicestershire examples, the usual story is that a piper or fiddler and his dog set off along an underground tunnel. Those on the surface follow his progress by the sound. After a while there is no more music and a few moments later the dog comes back to the surface very frightened. The musician is never seen again. In some debased way, such legends seem to have derived from the belief that wells and other underground cavities are entrances to the Otherworld, and the place to start shamanic-style spirit journeys.

Take the next right. Follow to a poorly signed sharp left bend. Ignore the right turn on the bend and take the next right to:

LONG CLAWSON

There is a dramatic view over the Vale of Belvoir and Trent valley before the road descends the hill into the village. A restored windmill can be seen prominently on the left.

Turn left at the T junction and follow through the village until you reach the church (129:722272).

Perhaps best known for the Stilton cheese factory to the west end of the village, Long Clawson deserves to be better known for this fine church. Dedicated to St Remigius, the Norman pillars in the transcept under the central tower reveal that the original Norman church had a cruciform plan, although the present building, mostly of the thirteenth century, has the more conventional aisled nave.

There are various interesting carvings. On the south porch there is a tongue-poker and an animal with distinctly pointed ears. Inside the north aisle are four heads in a similar style to the porch. Three are animals - one with sprouting foliage, a 'Green Animal'. The north-west one is female, with a square headdress. There are several foliate carvings with small faces on the arch springers. Inside the central tower crossing are several heads. One is badly defaced, another female and a third again with pointed ears.

To the south-west of the church is the manor house. This has a large stone outside, presumably used as a mounting block. The owner informed me that legend tells of an underground tunnel between the house and the church. Such improbable tunnels - often of much greater length - are, again, quite common in folk traditions.

Medieval earthworks can be seen in the field to the east of the church.

Return through the village and leave by the the north-east, heading for:

HOSE

Take the first left in the village, at a small triangular green.

The church here (129:736293) is also dedicated to St Michael and All Angels, but we know that this is a comparatively recent re-dedication. Anglo-Saxon remains were found when excavating, but apart from the general appearance of the fourteenth century building with sixteenth century clerestory, perhaps the most interesting aspect is the font which rests on four angels with outspread wings and between them are four faces, of which two have a sun-burst appearance.

On the outside, at the east end of the chancel window are two animalistic heads, the right hand one a tongue-poker. There are a few other heads including four gargoyles on the tower.

Follow around the village (turn left before the Post Office to avoid a poorly-signed dead-end) and continue on the lanes to the north-east to:
HARBY
Take the first right in the village and then left into School Lane.

A fragment of an old cross is now part of the war memorial just past the school (746312).

Car drivers should park by the cross and follow the signed footpath to the church, which is somewhat separate from the village (129:747313).

Dedicated to St Mary there is another interesting font with a variety of styles of tracery. Although 1606 is carved on it, this must refer to a restoration as it is in fourteenth century style.

In the nave are corbelled heads, including one girning with just one hand. On the outside of the tower are many small carvings including what might be two dragons.

Return along School Lane and take the lane to the east. Turn right to just past the railway bridge to:
STATHERN
Pronounced 'stat'hern', this name derives from the Old English for 'thorn stake' which could imply a boundary post.

Follow into the village, turning right at the give way, and take Red Lion Street then Church Lane. Car drivers should be careful and considerate if parking in the narrow and twisted street by the church and may find it easier to pull up in Red Lion Street.

The church is dedicated to St Guthlac - the enigmatic mercenary-turned-hermit who survived various torments by demons to found Croyland Abbey in Lincolnshire. In later years he was accused of immoral living and was murdered by his own bodyguard. The man who took over his cell was a pagan, which raises all manner of impenetrable questions over the origins of Croyland Abbey. At Stathern a portrayal of St Guthlac in stained glass forms the left-hand part of the east window - complete with lurid red dragon.

The font is again fourteenth century although is is greatly predated by the fragment of an Anglo-Saxon cross shaft. The north nave wall has carvings of demonic males, with perhaps a pair being horned or with hare-like ears. One is a face-puller (but strictly not 'girning' as he is not using his hands). On the south side are female heads. Outside the church look out for the scratch dial and the tower gargoyles. One is clearly girning; another is in a sheela-na-gig (female exhibitionist) posture.

Dalliwell Lane and Dolly Well House attest to the former location of the Dalliwell. This is an unusual name and, if not a suggestion that the women collecting water dallied there gossiping, then it might be a corruption of 'halliwell', a common form of 'holy well'.

Go back out of the village by the lanes to the north-west and (unless you want to take in the far-from little-known Belvoir Castle) turn right onto the long straight road and take the third left into:

REDMILE

The church of St Peter's is close by the disused Grantham canal (129:796355) and again has Anglo-Saxon carvings - this time a tombstone decorated with interlace reused as a windowsill by the pulpit. There is also one Norman pillar. The rest is basically thirteenth or fourteenth century in style but heavy-handedly restored.

Outside, there are no less than twelve gargoyles on the tower, one on each of the corners and two on each face. One on the south side is a contortionist with his head between his legs and the lead spout forming his 'delicate' parts. On the north is a lion, on the west a girning face. There are various small heads up the side of the spire.

In the graveyard are flourishing yews and many fine Swithland slate tombstones, including several with the distinctive 'Belvoir angel' motif, which is otherwise elusive in the Vale (see illustration page 31).

Return to the crossroads to the south-east and turn left. Cross the bypass and enter:

BOTTESFORD

In the centre of the village can be seen the old stocks and whipping post, by the side of the stump of a fourteenth century cross.

Perhaps the church of St Mary the Virgin (130:807392) should not be considered as 'little-known', being the biggest Leicestershire village church with the highest spire (at 210 feet). In some ways it is the Westminster Abbey of the midlands, having an overwhelming collection of sepulchral effigies to the Earls of Rutland that quite takes over the chancel.

Take time to also look at the arch springers in the nave. These make up a menagerie of three-dimensional carved animals and an upside-down 'falling man'.

The 'witchcraft tomb'

One of these Bottesford monuments (the triple decker at the south-east of the chancel) bears an inscription which records that the two sons both died in their infancy 'by wicked practice and sorcery'. The circumstances led to Joan Flower of Langham and her two daughters, Margaret and Phillipa, being brought to trial in 1619 at Lincoln Assizes. Joan was reputed to be a witch and Phillipa had allegedly bewitched one Thomas Simpson when her amorous advances were declined. The other daughter, Margaret, entered the service of the Duke of Rutland at Belvoir Castle but was dismissed for stealing.

As a result Joan, with her daughters and three other women, cursed the earl and his family. They procured a glove belonging to the youngest son, Henry, and performed various magical acts including dipping it in hot water and pricking with pins. Henry died in 1613. A glove belonging to the next son, Francis, was subjected to further magical deeds and buried in a dunghill. He became ill and, indeed, after the trial he died, in 1620.

Either on the way to gaol or actually inside Joan asked for some bread and butter, announcing that if she was guilty then God would strike her down there and then. She did indeed die after taking a mouthful, although the more prosaic explanation is that she was well aware of her likely fate and used the opportunity to take poison. The others were tried and found guilty. It is generally believed that Margaret and Phillipa were hanged, although no records survive from Lincoln assizes for this period.

All these carvings are difficult to date, although most are probably of the sixteenth century. Do not miss the corbel between the north door and north transcept which has a head with what is perhaps intended to be a dragon crawling out of the mouth. Over the pulpit on the chancel arch wall is a one-eyed (or maybe three-eyed) monstrous human face.

The base of the font has eight heads, all tongue poking. High up in the nave clerestory there are also tongue pokers in the arch springer. One also has pointed ears giving the impression of a beaked head. Apart from the carvings, look out for the traces of a medieval wall painting above the chancel arch.

Outside there are superb gargoyles on the south side - both above the aisle and the nave wall. One is a bell ringer. Was he the result of a prevalent fear of witches in the Vale and the belief that 'Witches could not fly when the church bells were ringing'? There is also a scratch dial. Take a walk around the graveyard and notice how this sits attractively along the rivulet.

Three Shire Oak

To the north of Bottesford parish is the meeting place of the counties of Leicestershire, Nottinghamshire and Lincolnshire. Although no longer surviving, this was marked by the Three Shire Oak and the Star Stone.

The late eighteenth century antiquarian Nichols tells us: 'At the north extremity of the parish, the three counties of Leicester, Lincoln and Nottingham, meet at a place called The Three Shire Bushes (a thorn bush in each county) near which is an upright stone with the figure X; at which place, during the perambulations of parishes, after prayers by the clergyman, were various sports for children; but within these twenty years discontinued, as the inclosures have rendered perambulations less necessary.'

Those intrigued by alignments of ancient sites may be interested that Three Shire Oak and the churches at Muston, Woolsthorpe and Harston all align.

If you have time, drive on towards the level crossing on the track to the north-east of the village (130:810393) and park up. Follow the track to the top of Beacon Hill (130:813397).

For such a slight climb it is surprising how good the views are on a clear day, and obviously suited to its one-time role as a beacon site.

Take the old main road south-east, doglegging left then right over the new A52 to:

MUSTON

Place-name origins are again intriguing - this deriving from 'mouse infested town'!

The church of St John the Baptist is attractive and agreeably situated (130:829378) although offering no curious carvings or other enigmatic features. Like most of the churches in this part of the county, it is mostly thirteenth and fourteenth century apart from the fifteenth century clerestory and font.

Muston cross

Turn right (south-west) at the church and then left.
The road goes past a most elegant market cross on the village green (130:828376).
The road takes you into Lincolnshire then over a disused canal. Take the first right to Woolsthorpe and continue through directly into:
HARSTON
Go over the crossroads in the village and turn immediate right, a narrow entrance signed to the church.
Harston is another fascinating place-name, deriving from 'hoar stone', meaning 'old grey stone', although no such stone is now known. Perhaps it stood on the Leicestershire-Lincolnshire border, which is still marked by an ancient trackway now called the Drift or Sewstern Lane.
The church is dedicated to St Michael and All Angels (130:838318) and sits on a hilltop with good views of Belvoir Castle. It is partially fourteenth century although the rebuilding of 1871 and 1888 is more prominent. In the porch is a fragment of Anglo-Saxon cross shaft with superb interlace decoration. Fragments of other Anglo-Saxon cross shafts have been embedded into the outside wall of the east end of the chancel. Evidence for Anglo-Saxon occupation has been found about a quarter of a mile south of the village, and a small cemetery towards Knipton.
Return to the crossroads. On the left corner is a curious structure in the wall, presumably a disused pump or well.
Leave by the lane heading west for Knipton which has some interesting thatched cottages and a partly-thirteenth century church. Go past the disused pump with its timber and tile roof. To the south-west of the village take the minor lane towards:
BRANSTON
Turn right in the village to the church (130:810295).
Another dedication to St Guthlac and another thirteenth century building although the font is Norman, decorated with architectural arcading. There is a gilded wooden reredos of the Last Supper. Outside, look out for the scratch dial and the many gargoyles which include another bell ringer, a bagpiper and what appears to be a tongue-poker.
Take the lanes south (signed to Melton) and turn left on the A607 to:
CROXTON KERRIAL
Pronounced to sound something like 'croe-ston'. On the right is Croxton Park where there was once a Halliwell ('holy well') and there are still oak trees about 500 years old.
Take the second left in the village to the church of St John the Evangelist and St Botolph (130:835295) on its prominent hill top site.
This is worth visiting for some fine fifteenth century bench-ends.

43

Leave the village by the lane leading south then turn left (signed Wyville) which will bring you to:

KING LUDD'S ENTRENCHMENTS

What should be visible here is a substantial length of Anglo-Saxon double-ditched boundary earthwork and about a dozen burial mounds which originate in the bronze age but were reused some 2,000 years later in the Anglo-Saxon period. Instead there is only a short length of the earthwork, hidden in dense woodland, and one

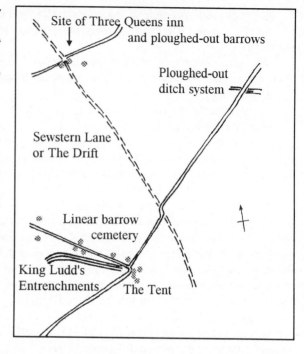

surviving barrow, also in a wood. The rest have been ploughed away, although two of the barrows were excavated before being totally lost.

The Anglo-Saxon boundary earthwork is known as King Ludd's Entrenchments, although it is very unlikely that this mythical king had anything to do with their creation. King Ludd is said to be buried in the tumulus in the wood to the east of the road (130:867279) which is known as The Tent. Note that all these sites are on private land and cannot be seen from the road.

Take the lane to the south-west past the remains of buildings associated with the wartime airfield to:

SALTBY

St Peter's sits by the crossroads (130:857249) with excellent views in all directions. Curiously, the nave and chancel are not exactly east-west, but about 80^0. There are eight gargoyles on the tower including a one-handed girning face on the west side. Inside the nave are twelve corbel heads, rather plain but distinctly male and female in character. The one nearest the chancel on the south side is probably a bear in harness, but may be a horse. The roof bosses are a mixture of leaf designs and human heads.

Although now overgrown and neglected, there is still a chalybeate spring, the water of which is dark brown and comes out frothy, rather like beer (130:844261).

44

If a lunch break is needed, the Nag's Head pub in the village can be recommended for excellent food. *Otherwise, take the road south to:*

SPROXTON

Pronounced 'sproe-ston'. Pull into the church of St Bartholomew (130:857249) on its hill-side location away from the present village and admire the splendid and nearly-complete Anglo-Saxon cross shaft outside. The carving is worn away on one side (it was used as a footbridge over a stream for who-knows how long) but on the other faces interlace decoration and a dragon can be made out. It is probably ninth or tenth century in date.

On the tower are four gargoyles, the north-east one is a griffin-like animal with 'bug' eyes that is girning. On the vestry is a tongue-poker with pointed eyes, but probably of nineteenth century date.

Although normally locked, the key can be obtained from the village. This is well worth the trip there and back as inside the nave are some superb carvings. Unique in the county - and probably much further afield - are six large wooden carvings of Green Men. One even has foliage sprouting from his eyes. Although now lacking the paint which would originally have made them resplendent they are among the least-known yet most magnificent carvings that I have yet discovered in Leicestershire and Rutland.

Also in the nave are sixteen superb corbel heads. On the north side three have pointed ears. One of these is girning, another is tongue-poking. One is also a dragon and a beaked head. In the south-east corner is a hedgehog. Altogether Sproxton is a quite undeservedly little-known treasure house of sculpture.

Sproxton cross (from Nichols)

The lane leading west from Sproxton (first right in the village) goes through:

STONESBY

St Peter's (130:823247) is late thirteenth century with a Norman font which has been recut at a later date. Among the corbels is a Green Man.

Rejoin the lane westwards to return to Waltham on the Wolds.

Sproxton Green Men

Tour 4 North-east of Leicester

A surfeit of stones

OS Sheets 129, 140 & 141
Approximately 36 miles

HUMBERSTONE

By the side of roundabout on the Troon industrial estate, rather inconspicuous except for the surrounding timber fence, is the remains of an eight foot high sandstone boulder, Leicestershire's best-known standing stone (140:62430710). Although these days referred to as the Humberstone, after the nearby village. The currently-accepted derivation is from *Humbeart's stan* (stone). In historical documents it is referred to variously as Hoston, Hell Stone or Holy Stone; the last two being closely linked linguistically.

The stone stands towards the top of a hill which has clear views to the west, including Old John. What is left of the stone is now almost totally buried. Until at least 1750 it stood in an artificial hollow. The broadest side faces north. It is made of a granitic rock which may have been moved, in part at least, by glacial action.

No one who interfered with the stone had good fortune. A prosperous eighteenth century farmer who broke a large fragment from the stone died in the parish workhouse six years later. It was believed that fairies inhabited the stone. One man heard a deep groaning and ran away, 'terrified lest he should see one of its unearthly inhabitants.'

'There is a legend that it was dropped by one of the old gods. No excavations have yet been made, due to the strong feeling that misfortune followed anyone who interfered with it. Mr William Anne Pochin of Barkby, the owner, started investigating. He met with an accident and shot half his hand off. . . . The Holy

> The fields east of the Humber Stone were known as 'Ost End', the other side being called 'West End.' One plot is known as 'Hell Hole Furlong'. Fields known as 'Hell Holes' are known in other parts of England; there are Upper and Lower Hell Holes at Whissendine and the south-west corner of Burbage Wood is also known as Hell Hole. Most place-name experts regard the term as a derogatory one, presumably indicating difficult soil. However, *hell* and *hole* are both also encountered as a derivation of 'holy'.

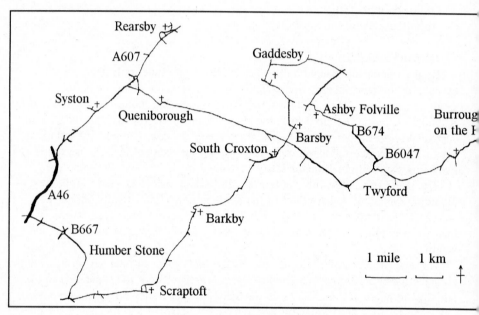

Tour 4 - starts Humber Stone

A photograph of the Humber Stone taken just before 1908.

Stone is still the fairies dancing ground, at least it was so fifty years ago. I have never seen them myself but my nursery maid had known people who had and so did Mrs Leatherland the blacksmith's wife, and the farmer who ploughed too close up to it lost all his money and died in the workhouse, so, it must be true.'

(From *Leicestershire* by Guy Paget and Lionel Irvine. Robert Hale 1950.)

Tradition also holds that it was the site of a nunnery - although there is no documentary evidence for such an establishment - and, even more improbably, of an underground tunnel all the way to Leicester Abbey.

Head off north-west and turn right onto the A46. At the first roundabout take the third exit into:

SYSTON

Syston was once described as a 'desperately uninviting industrial village'; the redevelopment of the town centre shops and a bypass have done something to alleviate the problem. History can be found if one knows where to look, as a brick house dated 1686 in Brook Street is considered to be the earliest surviving all-brick house in the county.

Proceed to the town centre. Turn left at the mini roundabout into High Street. Take the first right (Upper Church Street) and pull up on left.

St Peter's church (129:627118) is of thirteenth century origin but rebuilt 1870-80. There are gargoyles to be seen on the tower, relatively modern faces and figures on the aisles and an older frieze of small faces on the chancel. Note also the unusual font with ten sides.

Inside are beautifully carved fifteenth century panels on the six-sided pillars dividing the nave from the aisles, and around the chancel arch. The nave roof has particularly fine medieval carved bosses with supports carved as angels holding shields; other angels holding musical instruments support the north aisle roof.

The angels in the nave stand on stone corbels of an earlier date. Uniquely in the county (to my knowledge) these stone faces have been restored to their original painted condition. Whether the colours are quite as the originals we will never know (I suspect that medieval tastes would seem garish to modern eyes) but those interested in medieval carvings should visit Syston just for the experience of seeing this style of corbel painted.

Turn back to the mini roundabout and turn left, taking the old main road north-east to join the A607 through the edge of East Goscote and enter:
REARSBY
Turn left at the first crossroads (just past the Horse and Groom pub).

Note the many interesting timber-framed buildings. However, the timber-framed house dated 1613 was built this century, using old materials.

Around the bend and near a farm yard with cob walls on the other side of a brook, pull up by the minor track. The Blue Stone stands by the corner of the track (129:649145). Near here is a seven-arch packhorse bridge dating from the fifteenth century.

Turn left at the junction by this bridge and take the next left, then first left into Church Leys Avenue. Pull up at the end and head for the church to the north-east (651146). From the street a yew-lined path takes you through the churchyard.

There are interesting slate tombstones, especially one from 1660 and another which commences: 'A fatall knife his mortal body flew . . .'

Inside there is fourteenth century north arcade.

Return along Church Leys Avenue, turn right then right at the give way. Follow around left at the bend near the packhorse bridge and then turn right onto A607 (take care - visibility is very restricted).
Return to the roundabout and turn left into:
QUENIBOROUGH
Turn left at give way and proceed along the main street of fascinating and picturesque houses.

Towards the end is St Mary's church (129:651120). The spire is one of the finest - in both senses of the word - in the county and is a recognisable landmark over a wide distance.

The church has a generally attractive interior. Hidden up in the west end of the nave roof is a wooden carving of a male exhibitionist. Well worth taking a high-powered torch with you as the light switches are extremely difficult to locate! There is a Norman window in the chancel and thirteenth century arcades.

Just a little further east is a dovecote dated 1705. This originally stood to the north-west of the church but was removed and rebuilt in the 1980s. Cross the small bridge to the east of the dovecote and to the right are two large fragments of stone (129:653121). These might be the fragments of a larger standing stone.

Continue eastwards for three miles and turn left at the crossroads into:

BARSBY

Before turning left at the crossroads in the village, look out for Godson's Folly. This was built in the shape of a church and intended as a mortuary chapel but never consecrated (it is now a house).

Having turned left in the village follow the lane then turn left onto the B674 (note tower of windmill to right) into:

GADDESBY

Turn right into Church Lane and follow to end.

St Luke's church (129:690130) is elaborately decorated, particularly the 'showpiece' south aisle. Everything dates to the period 1260 to 1360 and may have been financed by the Knights Templars as it was one of the churches forming the Peculiar of Rothley, where there was a Templar Preceptory.

Large numbers of stone faces inside and out, mostly straight-forward male and female pairs, are probably of the late thirteenth century. Some of these faces are tongue-pokers. The most pronounced of these is on the exterior of the window at the west end of the south aisle; its counterpart is clearly horned. In the north aisle facing the north door are more animated faces including what may be a bear wearing harness. Another north aisle face is human but grimacing and showing all its teeth.

On the outside of the north aisle are four gargoyles, the one nearest the north door is girning. The north aisle has heads and ball flower decoration which can be dated fairly closely to 1330-1350.

The church guide refers to a carving of a mermaid, but I regret not recognising anything fitting this description. While church guides usually omit all reference to their carvings, those that do venture to mention them often contain the most fanciful descriptions. However, I will reserve judgement and would be interested to hear from any visitors who do find the fishy lady in question.

No one entering the interior can fail to notice the overpowering near-life-size equestrian monument Colonel Cheney, who had four horses shot under him at Waterloo but went on to live until 1848.

Return to the main street and turn right. Take the lane by the side of the Cheney Arms. Turn right at the edge of the village (signed Great Dalby and Kirby Bellars). Take the next right and pull up at the next crossroads.

In the field to your right (the south-east) can be seen the Folville Cross (129:715134). This is a square shaft about three feet high on a square plinth. Early in the fifteenth century Eustace de Folville was killed in a duel. This cross marks the site. However, it also is said to mark a boundary so it remains unclear whether the boundary marker - a suitable place for convening a duel - came first or whether the boundary was defined around the existing cross.

*Carvings in
Ashby Folville*

Turn right and take the road south-west and into the village of:

ASHBY FOLVILLE

Turn left at the give way.

Ahead is the Carrington Arms which has, it is claimed, the most complex heraldic device appearing on a pub sign anywhere in the country. However, do not spend too much time outside as the interior is also very inviting. I have enjoyed the excellent ham, egg and chips on a number of occasions.

Suitably refreshed, head across the road to the church of St Mary the Virgin (129:706120) which is mostly fourteenth century. Keys can be obtained from the white-painted house to the west of the churchyard.

Some visitors will find the sepulchral effigies in the south chapel of greatest interest - especially as the fifteenth century alabaster ones have been superbly restored. Look out too for the cadaver in a shroud. Others will find the carved wooden angels in the roof to be even more outstanding. They are of a quality unique in the county and, it is claimed, still bear their original paint. One plays the bagpipes. The stand on stone corbels also carved with fascinating figures. On the roof bosses are foliate heads, although none have foliage sprouting from their mouths. Best estimates of date put the stone corbels at *c.*1220 and the roof bosses and angels at *c.*1520.

In the north-east of the nave by the chancel arch is a girning head. On the south wall of the nave is a twin-headed character with three eyes and a horned head. The Norman font is decorated with arcading and three small animal heads. In the floor of the north transcept, rather neglected and often covered with clutter, is the stone mensa - that is, the pre-Reformation altar. It can be identified by the consecration crosses.

There is a well-documented tradition of a hay strewing ceremony at Ashby Folville. The field from which the hay was brought for the ceremony was called 'The Bartholomews'. The hay was taken from a part of the field marked out by three stones, in a triangular configuration. The ceremony was discontinued in the 1890s. The stones and adjacent field boundaries are understood to have been removed.

Follow the B674 south-east to:
TWYFORD
At the give way turn right to join the B6047 then turn left after the bridge.

St Andrew's church (129:730101) has a Norman north arcade dated to 1175, and a thirteenth century font. There was a well near the church although I believe this is now filled in.

Continue on the minor road. This will bring you through the village of:
BURROUGH ON THE HILL
St Mary's church (129:757108) has a scratch dial. Inside, the arcades and chancel are thirteenth century, as is most of the building, including the font decorated with skulls and faces. There is an effigy tucked away too.

Continue through the village. On the ridge to the left will appear the prominent ramparts of:
BURROUGH HILL FORT
The car park entrance is on the left at the right-hand bend. A short walk provides access to the hill fort (129:760120).

This is the best-preserved iron age hill fort in the county, indeed in much of the Midlands, with the ramparts still up to twenty feet high. Protected by sheer slopes on three sides these were complemented by strong fortifications on the fourth side - a ditch and massive rampart. Excavations revealed this was faced with drystone. In the south-east corner (also the entrance nearest the footpath) is an inturned entry. Excavation revealed evidence of strong masonry and a cobbled roadway. Little excavation has taken place in the interior and no huts have been found but there are many storage pits and finds of pottery, querns and animal bones.

Although abandoned in Roman times it remained in importance and horse races, fairs and festivals were held here until the eighteenth century. Even the Grand National was run here in 1873.

The views are especially impressive. A toposcope on the north-west bank provides some clues to the surroundings.

Return through Burrough village and into Twyford. Turn left at the B6047 and proceed up the hill. At the top turn right. This will return you to the crossroads near Barsby. This time turn left into:

SOUTH CROXTON

St John the Baptist church (129:692103) has gargoyles on the tower. One is girning and the south-facing one is bear-like. Another carved face has been set into the west end of the south aisle wall.

The church does not point east-west, but at 80^0. Some have suggested that this means the church was built to align with the sunrise on the patronal saint's feast day. However, St John the Baptist is associated with midsummer - and then the sunrise is further north. At least, it would be over a level horizon. Hills rise to the east of the church, however and would delay the sunrise. It is now more-or-less impossible to check this out as modern houses intervene.

Inside there is a Norman font decorated with arcading and a moustached face. To the north of the churchyard it is fairly easy to make out a medieval moat.

Continue through the village and where the houses peter out take the lane on the left into:

BEEBY

On the left, just after the little bridge and about fifty yards before you reach the church, is a stone truncated pyramid about five feet high with a pump in front (141:663083) known usually as the Holy Well. According to Nichols' illustration in the eighteenth century there was a more typical small structure with pitched roof. He also says the well was known as the Stockwell and has 'excellent mineral waters'.

The present structure is dated 1855 on the road side, above a padlocked steel door (see illustration on page 3). On the south side, facing the village, are two plaques:

'This well was restored in 1953 to commemorate
the coronation of Queen Elizabeth II.'

In summer's heat and winter's cold
One constant temperature I hold.
When brooks and wells and rivers dry
I always yield a good supply.
My neighbours say I'm often told
I'm more than worth my weight in gold.

Beeby church and well (from Nichols)

All Saint's church (141:664083) is basically thirteenth century and retains its font from this date. Slightly later is the mid-fourteenth century screen. The chancel is nineteenth century, as I suspect are the unusual and strikingly-carved figures in the nave arcade. There is a skull and cross bones and the 'mystical' symbol of a serpent crucified on a cross.

On the outside of the church can be spotted a girning gargoyle. The short spire - 'Beeby tub' - has a local legend attached to it concerning the two brothers who were the masons. They had successfully built the splendid needle-like spire at Queniborough but while at work on the steeple at Beeby they quarrelled over the cost and the ability of the tower to bear the steeple's weight. Eventually their ill temper resulted in a tussle and they ended up falling to their deaths. The spire remained as a stump.

The tale is also told in rhyme:

Beeby tub was to have been a spire.
Two brothers fought and broke their backs,
And so 'twas built no higher.

Continue south-west to:
SCRAPTOFT
Turn right at the give way just before the houses. Follow the one way system to All Saint's church (140:648056).

This has a thirteenth century cross with a square fluted shaft. The head is badly eroded and originally had a lantern top. The font is also of this century although the rest of the church is fourteenth century in style. The corbels in the chancel and nave are especially interesting. Superb-quality slate tombstones to the Wigley family with deeply-incised heraldry are now set into the chancel floor.

In the graveyard are slates to three generations of the Firmadge family. One is to the wife of W. Firmadge and three infants with a rare depiction of Charity.

From here it is easy to return to the Humber Stone or the centre of Leicester.

Scraptoft cross

56

Tour 5 East of Leicester

A feast of fine crosses

OS sheets 140 & 141
Approximately 16 miles

Although not one of the longer tours, cyclists should be aware that it takes in the highest village in Leicestershire and several other hill top locations. For the less-fit cyclist it might prove strenuous, especially on a windy day.

Families considering cycling outings should be aware that this route includes a short section of the busy A47 and is not suitable for children.

If starting from the city, then head to the east and follow the brown signs to the Farm Park. While not appropriate to the main theme of this book, there is no reason for not including the varied attractions of this children-friendly venue to the day's activities.

STOUGHTON

The village is to the east of the Farm Park. St Mary and All Saint's church is a prominent landmark in the centre (140:640021). Most of what can be seen is the result of a rebuilding in 1862, including the exceptionally large windows. Gargoyles on tower have snake-like spouts in their mouths. The north-east one is girning around its spout. A winged dragonesque beastie is depicted in the north-west corner.

In the churchyard is a beautiful fourteenth century cross with a moulded shaft ending in a capital with foliate decoration; no doubt originally surmounted by a now-lost finial. The circular stepped base is modern. Note that on three sides the churchyard is level with the top of a retaining wall about three feet high.

Head south-west from the church and take the lane east around the south side of the aerodrome.

This is the course of the Roman Road known now as the Gartree Road. On your left will appear a farm. This is:

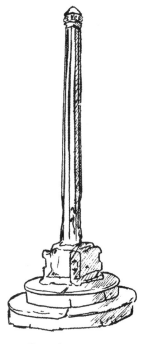

Stoughton cross

57

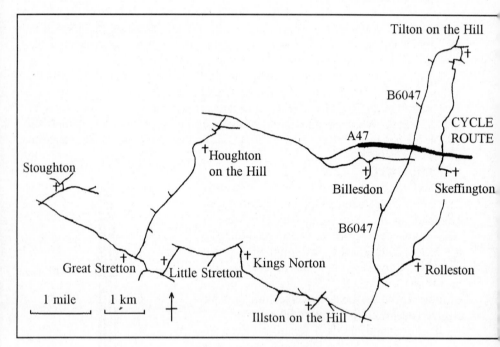

Tilton on the Hill

B6047

A47

CYCLE
ROUTE

Stoughton

Houghton
on the Hill

Billesdon

Skeffington

B6047

Great Stretton

Little Stretton

Kings Norton

Rolleston

1 mile   1 km

Illston on the Hill

Tour 5 - starts Stoughton

GREAT STRETTON

The church is tucked back on the right (141:657005). 'Great' Stretton long ago became what are known to aficionados as a 'DMV'. This abbreviation is for 'deserted medieval village' and Leicestershire has about 70 of these. (There are various reasons why they became deserted; often the succession of plagues of the fourteenth century may have been a factor but, contrary to popular opinion, the Black Death alone is rarely the sole cause - greedy landowners evicting their tenants often play a big part.) The humps and hollows to the far side of the church are the remains of streets and house platforms. There is also a moated manor site to west of church.

St Giles' church stands on the crest of the hill. Although rebuilt in 1838 various fragments of Norman carving are set higgledy-piggledy in the walls. The font is another of these examples of fourteenth century sculpture displaying intricate tracery designs.

Take the first left, the lane heading north-east which takes you directly into:

HOUGHTON ON THE HILL

Although modern houses now obscure the views, St Catherine's church (141:676033) occupies the summit of the hill and the spire is visible over a wide distance. It is basically a fourteenth century building, although the font is probably thirteenth century and is decorated with faces. On the outside is a scratch dial.

Nichols informs us that 'About 100 yards from the church there is a fine spring of water, very warm in summer, and cold in winter.' Two hundred years later the chalybeate water still flows. The well can be seen from the south-east corner of the churchyard, surrounded by three pollarded willows, and is on a footpath through the field (141:678033).

In the fields to the south and south-west of the church is prominent ridge and furrow plus another earthwork which may be deserted medieval house platforms.

Houghton on the Hill cross

59

Continue along the street and enter the main part of the village.
There is a prominent cross at a three-lanes end (141:680037). The base and shaft are modern but the lantern head is older.

At the north of the village turn right onto the A47 - cyclists should remain alert to the numbers of HGVs and caravan-towing cars which use this road.

To the north-east and clearly visible is:

BILLSDON COPLOW

This has a curious double-peaked appearance. Those who travel around Leicestershire will know that it is a distinctive landmark from high places around the north of the county. I frequently travel on the Fosse Way (A46) north of Leicester and Billsdon Coplow stands out clearly to one side, Charnwood Forest to the other.

Although there is no evidence of earthworks within the wood there have been occasional archaeological finds which suggest both bronze and iron age use. It would be an obvious choice for a hill fort. More speculatively, it may have been an Anglo-Saxon moot site, especially when one considers that it is intervisble with two known major hilltop administrative centres at Croft and Gumley.

Follow the A47 and after about a mile-and-a-half turn right to enter:

BILLESDON

A fourteenth century cross stands on the green known as the Market Place (141:720025). It is near where the A47 used to run until the village was by-passed. The terminal of the cross is small with fleur-de-lys mouldings, not big enough to have been the original head.

Rejoin the old A47 and continue up the hill to the T-junction at the summit. Turn left onto the B6047 and cross over the new A47 and follow north.

Billsdon Coplow is again visible on your left. To the right are the rounded hills of Whatborough and the curiously-named Robin a Tiptoe Hill. These two were once termed 'the motherly bosom of Leicestershire'.

Soon you will enter:

TILTON ON THE HILL

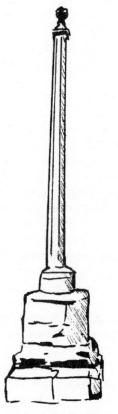

Billesdon cross

60

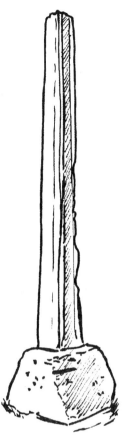

Tilton cross shaft

Turn right in the village and car drivers pull up before the church (141:743057).

This hill-top village is the highest habitation in Leicestershire. St Peter's church has a Norman font and priest's door in the chancel. Although broken, the medieval cross shaft still stands about 12 feet high - all from one piece of rather shelly limestone.

Lots of carved heads abound, inside and outside the church. Outside there is a fine selection of grotesque animals acting as gargoyles to the aisles and nave. One might be interpreted as having his head between his legs, with prominent scrotum (akin to the equally ambiguous figure in the nave at Thorpe Arnold).

Inside, the wooden roof bosses include four foliate heads. Notice that the nave is offset about three feet from the centre line of the chancel.

There is a narrow lane running south from the village, parallel to the B6047. Although this has a large number of gates which need opening it is fun for cycling but not quick. To take this route, head south from the church, turn right at the T-junction then take the minor left turn just around the bend. Beware of the first gate which is at the bottom of a steep slope with slippery gravel or mud at the bottom!

Car drivers are recommended to return back along the B6047.

With either route, cross straight over the A47, remaining on the narrow track or the B6047 respectively. From the B road turn left at New Inn which takes you along a chestnut-lined drive to Rolleston. (Note, this misses Skeffington which is on the 'back road route' only.)

The back road route leads through:

SKEFFINGTON

The church of St Thomas à Becket (742026) is fifteenth century, although the chancel was rebuilt about 1860. The Tudor hall is reputedly haunted.

In Skeffington turn right (left if returning from the church!) at the small triangular green and then - through an interminable series of gates - directly to:

61

ROLLESTON

Like Skeffington, this hamlet has a curiously secretive, 'little-known' feel about it, partly attributable to the profusion of trees and high hedges. The highest is probably the twenty-feet high yew hedge around the Tudor hall.

St John the Baptist's (141:733004) church has a tower dating back to around 1200, the rest was rebuilt in the eighteenth century. A fine ancient cross stands in line with the south west end of the church. The fluted shaft is surmounted by an almost complete stone cross.

The avenue of chestnut trees takes you to the B6047. Turn left and then right at the next crossroads. Follow the lane, turn right at the give way, then first left a few hundred yards along.

ILLSTON ON THE HILL

The hill top location of the church is fittingly matched by the dedication to St Michael and All Angels (141:706994). Throughout England many hill top churches are dedicated to this dragon-slaying saint. It is thought that they may well be christianisations of holy hills previously sacred to Lugh. (I am aware, however, that several of the St Michael churches in Leicestershire, including some included in these tours, do not occupy dramatic settings.)

Immediately outside the south door of the church is the fragment of a medieval cross shaft.

The church lost its original thirteenth century charm when over-restored in 1867. However a scratch dial remains and the south nave has gargoyles including a girning face, as well as three fabulous but more recent beasties on the aisle roof beneath. The gargoyle over the blocked north door is in a sheela-na-gig type position.

Inside there is font on a triangular base that may be twelfth century with faces in each corner.

Note the remains of a pump in the field to the west of the church.

Take the lane heading west from the village and follow signposts to take the next left and then next right which will bring you into:

KINGS NORTON

Just for a change there is no cross shaft here. Instead St John the Baptist's church (141:689005) is a remarkable example of eighteenth century Gothic. Built between 1757-75 it is of national importance for the interior is unchanged.

However, do not miss another feature which is now unusual but must once have been more common. In the west wall of the churchyard is a well in an arched recess. It has obviously been rebuilt in recent years but the large stone basin (three feet deep by five feet wide) still exists. Like other wells in churchyard walls it may have its source closer to, or under, the church itself. One only has to visit, say, Ireland to realise that *all* churches once had a well associated with them. Whether this means that the church christianised an already hallowed site, or just that this made it a convenient site for such a building is something which can be endlessly disputed.

Near the church is a thatched garden shed and a Victorian post box in a wall. *Leave the village by the north and turn left to take the lane heading west. Turn right then first left (take care - when I researched this route there were skid marks from what had clearly been a particularly nasty collision at this junction). This will bring you into:*

LITTLE STRETTON

The church is tucked away after the first house on the right (668003). It is dedicated to St John the Baptist and is one of the small, slightly higgledy-piggledy but inherently charming churches. There are rebuilt late Norman south and north doorways. The tower is thirteenth century. Note that there are no windows in the north side.

Continue through the hamlet and turn right. Either take the right soon after to return to Great Stretton and Stoughton or keep left for Great Glen and the A6.

Little Stretton church

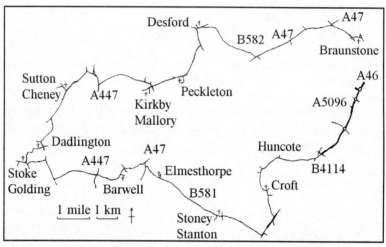

Desford

B582 A47

A47

Braunstone

Sutton
Cheney   A447

Peckleton

A46

Kirkby
Mallory

A5096

Dadlington

A47

Huncote

A447

Stoke
Golding

Barwell

Elmesthorpe

B4114

B581

Croft

1 mile 1 km

Stoney
Stanton

Tour 6 - starts Braunstone

Tour 6 South-west of Leicester

Mostly stones

OS sheet 140
Approximately 29 miles

BRAUNSTONE
Although time may have served Braunstone badly, the inter-war housing estate was built to the most adventurous ideas of its day - those which created the well-known 'garden cities' of Letchworth and Welwyn. Almost lost within this estate is the original settlement, with the church of St Peter (140:555029). It sits to one side of a large open area, in which can be discerned shallow traces of earthworks. Quite what this once was has never been investigated, but it is intriguing that there are a number of stones in the vicinity on both sides of Braunstone Lane - including one by the south porch of the church. However, despite its colour, one should not rush to the conclusion that this is the 'brown stone' which gave the village its name; rather defer to the place-name experts who deduce from the earliest forms of the name that it was 'Brant's tun' ('town').

The south porch is early eighteenth century, although the oldest part of the building is the Norman tower. The rest is no older than the last century and 1938 restorations.

The nearby B5418 will lead you north-west to the A47. Turn left and cross over the M1. At the cross roads with the B582 turn right.

This crossroads is shown on old maps as 'High Cross', suggesting a now-lost landmark. This is not to be confused with the High Cross which once stood at the junction of High Street and Highcross Street in the city, or with the High Cross which still survives at the south of the county where the Fosse Way crosses Watling Street.

The B582 takes you directly into:
DESFORD
Note the interesting brick and stone house on the left before the mini roundabout.

At the mini roundabout turn right into Main Street and pull up by the church.

Another curious stone lies near the church of St Martin (140:478034) but this time by inside the churchyard wall near the street. Note that the churchyard tends to be raised up as a mound. Although the church was mostly rebuilt in

1834 there is a Norman font decorated with a single row of beads. The gargoyle on the north-west corner of the tower is a rather unusual man's head.

The church is yet another of those which does not lie exactly east-west, but rather at 80⁰.

From the church return to the mini roundabout and head straight over, past an appealing row of old buildings. Almost immediately there is a turning hidden on the left - try not to miss it!

The correct road will go through houses before the Caterpillar factory appears. Just after the second Caterpillar entrance turn right and after a mile you will enter:

PECKLETON

The church is along the lane to the left (the turning is almost opposite the old building used as the village hall), where it sits remote from the present-day settlement neatly atop a small eminence, with only a rather attractive eighteenth century hall for company (141:470008). Tucked further away is the Manor House which has a moat and possible prehistoric barrow in the grounds.

The church is dedicated to St Martin and the oldest part is a Norman font. The building originates in the thirteenth century and has fourteenth century stained glass showing St Michael.

Outside there is a well-preserved scratch dial on the south aisle window frame. Looking south, Earl Shilton church is prominent on the skyline due south. During a visit some years ago a man tending the churchyard said that both churches were 'on the same level'. A quick look at the map revealed that this is true. However, it also suggested to me that this might be a folk memory of a deliberate alignment between the buildings. Indeed, there does seem to be a clear line of distinctive sites running due north from High Cross on the Fosse Way and Watling Street. I have described this in detail in *Putting things straight - aligned ancient sites in Leicestershire and Rutland* (Heart of Albion Press 1990; now out of print)

Return to the village and head left.

Out of the village you will pass under the cables of electricity pylons. Where they cross the road is a culvert (140:460007) which was known as Sherriff's Bridge and is probably the site of the Sparkenhoe Moot site - although Shericles Farm, nearer to Desford, is a corruption of the Old English for 'meeting-place oak tree' and could have been the venue instead.

Almost immediately you are in the village of:

KIRKBY MALLORY

Go straight over at the give way and continue into the cul-de-sac. Just before the entrance the the motor racing circuit, pull up. A small lytch gate marks the entrance to All Saint's church, which stands about a hundred yards beyond (140:454004)

The church is essentially fourteenth century and contains sepulchral effigies. *There is more than one way to get to the next site but the easiest to navigate is by taking the lane west from Kirkby Mallory (signed Market Bosworth) to join the A447. Turn right at the A447 and just past the petrol station turn left and follow the signs into:*

SUTTON CHENEY

Go past the Royal Arms and Hercules Inn. Turn right (signed Shenton).

St James' church (140:417005) is entered through a path between the outbuildings of the Almshouses tea shop, converted from seventeenth century almshouses. The church has a Norman font and arch although is otherwise of fourteenth century origin.

Those interested in fifteenth century warfare may want to divert to the Battle of Bosworth Country Park - although the sceptics among you may be interested to learn that scholarly research reveals that the site of the battlefield which is so earnestly promoted by Leicestershire Council is probably nothing more than an eighteenth century antiquarian's fancy. Details of an area nearer to Dadlington which much better fits the facts can be found in Peter Foss's book *The field of Redemore* (Rosalba 1990).

If not diverting, turn left from the Almshouse car park hen right at the give way, leaving Sutton Cheney by the lane to the south (signed Dadlington). Pass over Sutton Wharf Bridge over the Ashby de la Zouch Canal, then take the next left into:

DADLINGTON

In the village turn right at the T-junction, then left just around the first bend, into 'The Green'. Pull up just past the Dog and Hedgehog pub.

The little chapel dedicated to St James the Greater is on your left (rather hidden behind the hedge), sitting above a sharp drop. Although parts date to the early twelfth century the only figurative carvings look rather sixteenth century in style. The main interest is in the details of funding by Henry VIII which seems to be atonement for the lives lost during his father's victory at Bosworth field. It is claimed, no doubt correctly, that many of the dead from the battle were buried here.

Turn back into the village and follow signs for Stoke Golding. At the cross roads on the way out of the village turn right into Stoke Lane. The narrow lane will twist and turn but will take you past the White Swan pub and directly to the church at:

STOKE GOLDING

St Margaret's church is yet another of those splendours of Leicestershire which are quite unjustly little-known. About 1280-90 the masons indulged themselves in some totally fantastic capitals in the south aisle arcade. These are decorated with multiple faces, foliate heads, even a lady in a wimple, all amidst a forest of foliage. Perhaps the most curious depictions include a sideways face with big-ears and a tongue-poker.

The font is slightly later, perhaps about 1330, and depicts various saints including St Catherine herself, with her wheel, and St Margaret with a dragon. The timber roof bosses are fascinating too. In the south aisle is a tongue-poker with his head between his legs and an almost-girning face; the remaining bosses are foliate.

Outside there is a scratch dial and deep grooves in the windowsill of the south aisle to the west of the porch. These are caused by arrow sharpening. Romantically it has been suggested that these are the result of preparations for the Battle of Bosworth but, more prosaically, they are common on many churches and probably just reflect the statutory archery practice which took place every Sunday after church service.

The next site, Barwell church, is only a couple of miles due east but the route is best followed on the map. Continue from Stoke Golding church to the George and Dragon pub and turn left. Take the minor road almost immediately on the left (signed to Hinckley). Head east to the convent and school, then follow the road to the right (south-east). Turn left after about half a mile. Cross the A447 and take the B581 into:

BARWELL

Follow through the village, past the Red Lion then turn right (before the Three Crowns). Car drivers will see a spacious pull in by the church.

The village name seems to derive from 'boar's well' which might refer to the large pool in the field (High Close) near the hill top church (140:445968). The church itself is dedicated to St Mary and has a scratch dial. In almost all respects this is a complete fourteenth century church. Inside there is excellent modern foliate carving by men of village.

The largest recorded meteorite fall in Britain hit Barwell on Christmas Eve in 1965. It was preceded by hissing sounds and accompanied by loud acoustic phenomena.

Return and turn right to go past the Three Crowns.

The Queen's Head pub (on your left in the main street) is an interesting old half-timbered building. Outside is a large flat-topped recumbent stone; probably originally used as a mounting block, it is now well-polished from use as a seat.

At the mini roundabout go straight over and follow the B581 towards Earl Shilton but turn right at the A47 then immediate left to take the B581. This will lead into the small settlement of:

ELMESTHORPE

On the other side of the houses, and after a left hand bend and a farm entrance, there is a small lay-by on the offside of the road. Car drivers

Stoney Stanton tympanum

should park here, although be very careful of other traffic. The church is on your left.

Rather a curiosity these days, although before the extensive nineteenth century restorations quite commonly encountered among rural churches, the nave is ruined and only the tower and chancel are roofed. Inside is a late twelfth or early thirteenth century font.

Dedicated to St Mary (140:461965) it is said to have been the sleeping place of Richard III on the night before Bosworth.

Continue along the B581, over the M69, and enter:

STONEY STANTON

Outside a modern factory on the left (owned by Labesco in 1994) is a massive standing stone (140:486949). No doubt a modern 'memorial' to the extensive quarrying which characterises the area, by 'coincidence' the two flat faces align east-west and north-south in the manner of more timeworn examples.

Car drivers turn left into Nock Verges and park.

St Michael's church (140:489948) is attractive but the most exciting feature is now above the priest's door on the north side of the chancel. It is a Norman tympanum depicting various fighting dragons and beasts, a large bird and a crozier-brandishing bishop. The slot between the bird and the cleric is later damage. 'What is the meaning of this barbarity?' asks Pevsner and it is a difficult question to answer convincingly.

By way of a few clues, consider the function of the bird (sometimes, quite unconvincingly, described as a 'dove'). The Celts believed the world to be haunted not by sweet-singing Otherworld birds but by malevolent bird-flocks in the service of hostile gods. Comparatively recently death was thought of as coming in the form of a bird, sometimes a great black screaming night bird. Up until recently ravens were regarded as a favourite familiar of witches.

Look out for the peculiar double chimney at the rear of a brick-built house to the south-west of Nock Verges.

Continue along the B581 to the south-east and turn left at the B4114 (the Roman Fosse Way). Just before the dual-carriageway starts look to your left for a good view of Croft Hill (see below). At the crest of the hill in front turn left and follow into:

CROFT

Drop down to the bridge with the phone box and Heathcote Arms opposite. Turn left then immediately take the sharp 'dogleg' right turn. Pull up for the church.

Another St Michael dedication, this time sitting below the hill (140:511960). Apart from one Norman window in the west wall of the north transcept wall, the rest is from 1879. Inside there is a square font with plain palm-like upright leaves.

From near the church is a footpath which runs through a narrow verge of woodland around the western side of Croft Hill. (There is no better place to park so leave cars or bicycles near the church.)

The real interest Croft is the hill - assuming the quarry company refrain from blasting the surviving half into roadstone-sized fragments. Although discouraged by the quarry owners, access to the summit is a customary right of way. Although quite a modest height, less than 400 feet above sea level, it is by far the most substantial hill in this area. From the top there are distant views to an almost-flat horizon with only the hills of Charnwood Forest to the north. From the summit one also has the opportunity to look down into the enormously deep quarry operations which have removed the eastern half of the hill.

Croft Hill is known to have been used as an early christian meeting place, a fair site and an Anglo-Saxon judicial court. Recent exploratory archaeological activity has revealed some late mesolithic and early neolithic pottery plus some Roman and Saxon pottery sherds. There was speculation by an eighteenth century antiquarian that the hill fitted accurately the description of the Druidic 'omphalos' of England but this suggestion risks opening up a vast debate on places identified as sacred centres.

On firmer ground, one of the few surviving Anglo-Saxon documents relating to Leicestershire states that King Wiglaf of the Mercians held court here in 836. From the signatures on a surviving land grant it seems that the people attending where a who's who of ninth century England - including the Archbishop of Canterbury. This, along with secondary evidence, suggests that Croft was at that time the centre of a royal estate. Interestingly, one of the places intervisible from the summit is another known Anglo-Saxon royal estate centre at Gumley.

70

There is good reason for believing that forty thieves were tortured and executed here in 1124 (although it has been suggested that the site is near Syston).

Continue along the little street, past the Heathcote Arms.

As you drop down the main street, look to your left at the splendid mark stone. It stands about two feet above ground on a low retaining wall opposite what was presumably the old school house (140:513957). There was previously another stone in the village, although this is believed to have been lost.

Turn right, then right again at the phone box retracing your previous route briefly, but continue along the road into:

HUNCOTE

Continue through Huncote (signed Narborough) and past Red Barn Farm

Right by the roadside is a prominent stone which marks the boundary between the parishes of Croft and Huncote and, until at least the mid-1970s, was embedded in the side of a tree. Road improvements led to it being removed but local residents were successful in having it reinstated to its more-or-less original location.

Continue into Narborough and turn left at the B4114, the Fosse Way again. Follow under the motorway and straight over the roundabouts. The road changes designation to the A5096 and becomes a dual carriageway. Shortly the police headquarters will be seen on your right. At the next roundabout car drivers double back onto the south-bound carriageway (cyclists may dismount and walk across the busy road). Just to the south of the police HQ there is a service road set back on the east side; access is tricky and car drivers will find the entrance comes up quickly after the police station. Car drivers should park considerately in the access road then walk along the unmade lane heading east to the River Soar (see map overleaf). Under no circumstances should cars be taken along the track - the road surface deteriorates rapidly and there are no parking or turning places until the end. You are now in:

ENDERBY

The map will help guide you along the old green lane and towards the edge of the field by the loop of the river where (if the grass is short enough) one can find four small mark stones. These mark out an area of ground known as the Wether (that is, dialect for 'adult sheep').

There is a folk custom which once featured this little-known location. Every May there was a ritual auction for letting out the Wether. Anyone who wanted to bid must smoke a churchwarden pipe and could only bid while the tobacco

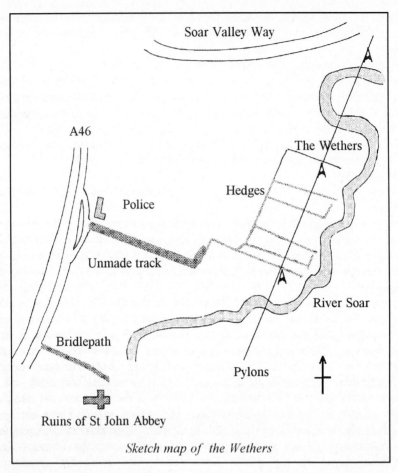

Sketch map of the Wethers

remained alight. At the end of the ceremony a nominal rent was enforced. More interestingly still, a procession took place from Enderby on Whit Monday. The hay from the Wether was carried in a straight line to High Cross in Leicester. Such ceremonies are known elsewhere and invariably involved high spirits and general fun making.

In a similar manner, at nearby Braunstone on the first Sunday in July hay gathered in Aylestone meadow was taken as the crow flies - without using pitchforks - to Braunstone church.

On the way back detour slightly to the ruins of a small church (140:553991). A tenth century carving was discovered here in 1952.

The Fosse Way (here the A5096 but soon changing to the A46) will take you towards Braunstone or to the city centre.

Tour 7 The Langtons and Market Harborough

Splendid carvings

OS sheets: 140 & 141
Approximately 32 miles (if you need to make this into a circular tour, note that the last place, Great Easton, is a further seven miles from the start).

MARKET HARBOROUGH

Although St Dionysus' church in the town centre and the adjoining grammar school of 1613 (141:733873) are not, I hope, little-known the same is not so certain for the ruins of St Mary in Arden up the hill from the railway station (141:739875). This was rebuilt in 1693 from a gale-wrecked predecessor but retains a Norman doorway with 22 beaked heads. Sheltering in the porch is the eroded effigy of a knight. The surrounding churchyard has some excellent slate tombstones. Perhaps one reason for the church's demise was a bad reputation for clandestine marriages and the 'ignorant and disorderly nature of its curates'.

The large sandstone block near the roadside is Peter's Pence Stone, also called Robin Hood's Stone. 'Peter's pence' refers to the taxation levied by the

Peter's Pence Stone by St Mary in Arden

73

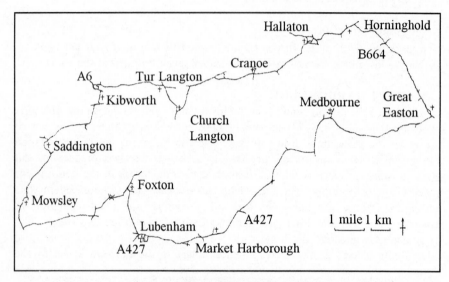

Tour 7 - starts Market Harborough

Vatican in pre-Reformation times. Interestingly, grave digging in 1799 revealed much earlier burials on the hill top site - a large Anglo-Saxon cremation cemetery.

There is a small but well-presented museum in the buildings behind the library and town hall offices.

Take the A427 west to:

LUBENHAM

Take the first left on the edge of the village (Old Hall Lane).

Although the present building is modern, you should be able to spot a moated house by the footpath (141:709872). Looking back towards the main road one might try imagining the late iron age encampment which survived until recent ploughing all but eliminated any traces.

Follow the lane around the corner and left at School Lane to the church.

Another moat is just to the south (141:705870).

The church is basically thirteenth century with a stubby fifteenth century tower. The interior is unrestored and has heads on the chancel arch.

Turn right at the corner of the churchyard and then left at the small green. At the A427 dog leg right, taking the road signposted to Foxton locks. Continue northwards. At the give way sign (at the interestingly named Gallow Field Road) turn left. Follow right into the village (ignoring directions to the locks). Pull up near the church.

FOXTON

St Andrew's church sits on a hill top with excellent views to the north (141:698897). It is late thirteenth century with a fourteenth century north porch. This has a hare-eared man and a crone-like woman with a square headdress. Inside there is a fragment of Anglo-Saxon cross shaft inside and a Norman font. Look to the east side of the churchyard and you will notice that the boundary is marked by a substantial length of cob wall. (there is another cob wall in Middle Street, at the end away from the canal.)

Return back towards Gallow Field Road and turn right,

Foxton hare-eared man

75

heading for the car park serving Foxton locks - which are most certainly not little-known!

Some readers will be aware of a previous Heart of Albion publication, *Around Foxton - memories of an Edwardian childhood,* by Sarah Dallaston (my maternal grandmother) in which she describes growing up in Bottom Lock Cottage (now the shop and pub) before the First World War.

Unless intending to visit the locks, drive past the car park and over the bridge. Turn immediately left and follow the little lane to a T-junction. Again turn left then turn right at the crossroads.

The farm opposite is Bunkers Hill Farm, which is where Sarah Dallaston spent her teenage years 'in service' helping make butter, pork pies, tend the fowls, and such like.

The road now rises along the ridge of the Laughton Hills. Ignore the turnings to the right and left and eventually, after about two miles, you will come to a T-junction. Pull up.

MOWSLEY

On the hill top to your left (south-east) near the hedge on the summit of the steep slope is hidden the Mowsley Stone (140:657877). This is a large recumbent stone nearly five feet long, aligned approximately north-west to south-east. The tapered end is highest, at two feet above present ground level. The sides all show a grey colour but the sloping top is a strikingly off-white colour.

Mowsley stone looking over to Theddingworth

76

It sits in a shallow depression, probably caused by animals trampling the soil into mud, and is not visible except when close to. The hill drops sharply to the south and there are good views towards Theddingworth. In Market Harborough Museum there is a photograph of the local historian and founder of Harborough Museum, Frank Strongman, standing by this stone, with the caption 'The Mowsley Stone was reputed to turn itself over when Theddingworth clock struck thirteen. As nobody has heard Theddingworth clock strike thirteen the theory has yet to be proved either way.'

Strongman located and photographed another stone nearby in the 1930s but the location he gave (at the foot of the ridge described above) is now a large ploughed field and presumably the stone was moved or destroyed.

Take the road to the right (north) from the T-junction into Mowsley village. Follow the road around bends in village.

St Nicholas church (140:647891) is thirteenth century with the relatively unusual cruciform plan. It has a scratch dial. Alongside the footpaths near the church are, at the time of writing, three fairly short lengths of cob wall although some are decaying rapidly.

Along a footpath to the north-west of the village can be found some substantial remains of medieval fishponds (140:646893).

Continue north. On the way you will encounter an enterprise common in many parts of England but almost unique in Leicestershire and Rutland - a rural tea rooms. If the thought of gateaux and other delights does not tempt you, proceed to:

SADDINGTON

Notice cob wall forming an outhouse just before the church.

St Helen's church (141:658917) has fourteenth century traces but was rebuilt in 1872. It stands on the ridge of a hill.

Take the first right after the Queen's Head. Proceeding through the village keep a look out for more cob walls. This road will take you on to and through Smeeton Westerby with its church of 1852. From here there is an almost imperceptible break in the houses before the outskirts of:

KIBWORTH BEAUCHAMP

Pronounced 'bee-cham'

Turn right at the T junction then left at the roundabout, with its splendid spreading cherry tree.

Just over the railway bridge one will see St Wilfred's church (141:685942). This is partly fourteenth century, the notable exception being the tower of 1832, and well worth a visit for its high-quality corbels in the nave. Just for once the church guide does give them a mention, indeed provides sketches. They include a girner and a tongue-poker. A pair of figures are prominently displayed on the chancel arch - the southerly one is distinctly girning; its counterpart is in an unusual Atlas-like position with his arms supporting the corbel block.

Outside look out for a scratch dial and a girning gargoyle and the east end of the south aisle. Also there are some good quality Swithland slate gravestones. I am told there is one with a distinctly buxom angle, but have not found her myself.

Proceed to the main A6 and turn left. Ignore the first right by the Rose and Crown pub and take the next right. Car drivers should pull up a safe distance away from the junction.

Walk back along the A6 to the footpath sign on the north side of the road. This will lead you to a little-known Norman castle mound or motte and bailey.

Return and set off eastwards along the lane.

A local historian has recently succeeded in locating many of the fragments of the old cross and restored it, near the pump opposite the impressive Georgian house.

Follow the road to the right and Kibworth Harcourt windmill (141:688945) will appear on the skyline. This road will take you into:

TUR LANGTON

The present church of St Andrew (141:714945) is of interest in that it is one of the few brick-built rural churches in the county, being built in 1866 to replace the old church of St Nicholas which stood to the north-west of the Manor House (only a thirteenth century doorway now survives).

Proceed into the village. By now I'm sure you're already keeping an eye open for cob walls and will spot the substantial length near the T-junction.

By the T-junction is a footpath which will take you in the general direction of King Charles' Well (141:722949). This was named after Richard I who, it is claimed, stopped there to drink on his campaigns. The present structure dates to 1813.

At the T-junction turn right towards:
CHURCH LANGTON
Turn left around triangular green and pull up by church entrance on left.

Another feast of medieval masons' imaginative carving awaits you at St Peter's (141:724934), with richly-imaginative

Double-head from frieze

friezes of faces and ball flower all around the north and south aisles. Among the heads look for one girning, two girning with one hand, a tongue poker, a Green Man (all these are on the north side) and a curious double-headed figure on one corner of the south aisle.

As the interior is well worthy of investigation, I hope that information on key holders to this church is now easily available, as I have been thwarted on a number of occasions in the past. Architecturally the magnificent clerestory gives a wonderfully airy feel. The most unusual carving is rather hidden in the passage to the vestry. It is probably early Norman and perhaps depicts the hammer god, Thor. Unfortunately the critical part of the carving is damaged and we do not know whether he holds a small cross or a hammer.

In the churchyard is a slate showing Adam and Eve with the Tree of Life and serpent. The figure of Death is directing a dart at Adam and the risen Christ is depicted below.

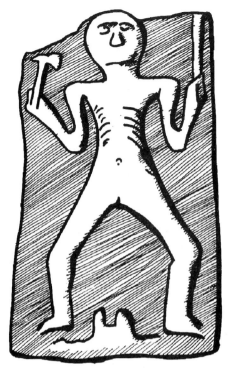

Church Langton man

The excellent Georgian rectory was built by William Hanbury, who combined the functions of rector with horticulturist, philanthropist and mild eccentric.

Leave the village by the lane leading north-east from the church.

At the bottom of the hill, rather lost in a clump of trees, is St Ann's Well (141:72729388). Now rather forlorn, with only traces of stonework suggesting this is more than a field drain, this was once the main water supply for Church Langton. It shares the same spring line as King Charles Well at Tur Langton.

Turn right at the T-junction and follow the road towards:

CRANOE

The hill top church is dedicated to St Michael (141:762953), although the structure mostly dates to 1849. Only the tower is thirteenth century.

Unless detouring to take in the church simply continue on the same road (being sure to keep left at the road junction on a bend) to take you into:

HALLATON

Pull up after church.

The church looms up over a massive retaining wall, quite appropriate for this is again dedicated to St Michael and All Angels (141:786965). In the porch is a splendid Norman tympanum of St Michael fighting with a dragon, with two small mere mortals looking on.

As one enters from the fourteenth century north porch a Green Man looks down from the north aisle corbels (see illusration page 16). In the church are a Anglo-Saxon tomb cover and a most wonderful Norman font with startling faces

---

Hallaton Easter Monday hare-pie scramble and bottlekicking

One of Leicestershire's most famous folk customs is the annual Hare Pie Scramble at Hallaton, as the event draws large crowds who take part in activities that make a rugger scrum look delicate.

One of the best descriptions is that of Charles Billson, writing at the turn of the century:

"On Easter Monday in every year a procession is formed in the following order:

"Two men abreast, carrying sacks full of hare pies.

Three men abreast, carrying aloft a bottle each, two of which are filled with beer and the third is a wooden dummy.

A hare (if it can be procured) in a sitting posture, mounted on top of a pole.

"The procession was also formerly accompanied by a man carrying a sack full of bread, which he threw out to be caught by the company.

"This little troop, followed by the townspeople and a band of music, marches to an ancient earthwork about a quarter of a mile south of the town, consisting of a small oblong bank with a narrow trench round it and a circular hole in the centre. This is known as 'Hare-pie Bank'. The pies are here tumbled out of the sacks and scrambled for by the crowd. Then begins the well-known 'Hallaton Bottle-Kicking'. The bottles containing the beer are first thrown into the circular hollow, and then the dummy bottle, for which all scramble, and the men of Medbourne or other villagers try to wrest it from the Hallatonians' grasp, and try to force it over the brook which forms the parish boundary."

(From *Leicestershire and Rutland: County Folk-lore,* 1895)

It has been suggested that the hare-pie scramble is the remnant of a rite in celebration of Eostre, who gave her name to the christian festival. Her sacred animal was the hare and Easter bunnies are evidence that traces of the old religions can survive in the twentieth century. In many parts of the country hares were regarded as witches' familiars and that by shape-shifting old crones could take the form of hares and return again.

Faces from Hallaton font

on the four corners. One face is 'column swallower', which may be some form of intentionally lewd symbolism. A second Green Man on looks down from a south aisle roof boss. Although now almost entirely blocked off, this church once had a crypt, which is quite unusual in the county.

A very minor track leads from the north side of the church and twists around the houses. This brings you to a T-junction. Turn left .

Fairly soon you will see the distinctive and well-preserved shape of a large Norman castle mound more-or-less below. This seems to be associated with extensive ironworking which was being undertaken in the vicinity at this time. Or it might be some reflection of the previous history, as we know that Hallaton was probably an Anglo-Saxon royal estate centre. However, excavations have revealed that the castle's moat has pre-Roman origins.

Return to the village.

Hallaton Hare Pie Procession in 1989

81

Hallaton's conical 'Butter Cross'

Leaving the church head for the middle of the village where there is a green on which are two crosses. One is obviously cross-like, the other a squat cone. The general appearance of the village makes it one of the prettiest in Leicestershire. There are four pubs in the village providing a range of refreshments.

Keep to the right of the green and past the Bewitch Arms. Follow left at the bend and then turn right (signed Horninghold). Soon after turn left and follow the lane to:

HORNINGHOLD

Coming in to the village, almost immediately on the right (although not easily seen from the road) is one of the best features of the village - St Peter's church (141:807972). There is a Norman south doorway with rows of stars, dove, a creature somewhat like a lion and 'demons' on capitals. Foliage sprouts from the mouths of the heads of the 'demons'. A fine dragon is carved on the left-hand capital. Also on the south side is a scratch dial.

Inside is a thirteenth century font, which is the date of most of the rest of the building, perhaps including the spire.

Continue along the road to the north-east then take the first right after about a quater mile. Cross the B664.

As the Eyebrook Reservoir comes into view on the left you are looking across the site of a lost medieval village which went by the intriguing name of Holyoaks. There is no direct evidence that this was a pagan Anglo-Saxon shrine but it is interesting that in nearby Ayston parish there is another Anglo-Saxon place-name which suggests a grove dedicated to the god Thor.

The thirty villagers living at Holyoaks in 1496 were evicted by Sir Robert Brudemell to make way for pasture.

Continue to:

GREAT EASTON

Take the first left in the village (Lounts Crescent). Pull up near the end.

The church of St Andrew (141:849933) has a late thirteenth century tower with heads. Look out for a scratch dial in the form of a full circle, which seems curiously at odds with the basic working principles. Furthermore, it faces south-west, not due south! Inside there are various heads on the arch springers and as corbels for the pre-clerestory roof. Perhaps the most notable are a foliate head on a capital of the north arcade and a small naked male figure in the east end of the nave. A substantial fragment of an Anglo-Saxon cross shaft was discovered quite recently. In the field near Rectory Farm is a curious structure known

Great Easton capital with foliate head

as Roman Well (141:850933). Ask at the farm for permission and directions. Although it is now quite dry, the remains of a ditch runs down towards the farm.

Return to the road through the village, turning left from Lounts Crescent. Go past the attractive ironstone buildings and turn right at the war memorial cross. At this end of the village are several pretty thatched ironstone cottages. This lane takes you south-west. Keep right at junction into Drayton. Follow through the village and along the Welland valley into:

MEDBOURNE

Turn right to where St Giles church (800931) stands on a mound above a ford; the churchyard is said to have been moated at one time. The Norman font is similar to Hallaton but has lost its heads. Medbourne was a Roman town and a mosaic pavement was discovered under what is now a private garden (it was reburied).

Retrace a short distance back onto the B664 which will take you through Northamptonshire towards Market Harborough.

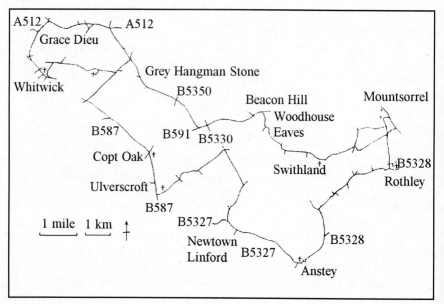

Tour 8 - starts Anstey

84

Tour 8 Charnwood Forest

Stones and hill forts

OS sheets: 129 and 140
Approximately 32 miles.
Includes two short walks where stout footwear will be essential in wet
weather.

ANSTEY

Although not one of Leicestershire's more picturesque villages, there are a
few timber-framed cottages. Over the Rothley Brook (140:553084) is an excellent
fifteenth century bridge. Just a field or two away (it is difficult to give more
helpful directions as, at the time of writing, the A46 Western Bypass is under
construction in the vicinity) is an intriguing standing stone (140:55260820). This
stands on the headland of medieval ridge and furrow, so almost certainly
predates it. Standing to south-west one can accurately line up the tower of St
Mary's church (140:550085) and the hill-notch (now wooded) beside Old John.
As Paul Devereux and Ian Thompson observed this is part of a longer alignment
from Oadby through Frog Island and on towards a deeply-moated hill top iron
age site near Belton (P.
Devereux and I. Thompson,
The ley hunter's companion
(Thames and Hudson 1979);
also discussed in
R.N. Trubshaw *Putting
things straight - aligned
ancient sites in
Leicestershire and Rutland,*
Heart of Albion Press, 1990;
now out of print) .

*Gynsall Lane stone (before being pushed
upright) looking to St Mary's and Old John.*

The stone was at a
pronounced angle, pointing
along the direction of the
alignment, until summer
1991 when the landowner
pushed it upright. Sometime
in the 1970s an amateur
archaeologist, Mike Kerr,
excavated around the stone.

While this disproved the local belief that it was as deep under ground as it was above, the only significant discovery was a 'blind' spring underneath.

Returning the village centre, note that St Mary's is on a pronounced mound and there is the remains of a circular cross shaft in the churchyard.

Follow the B5327 north-west to:

NEWTON LINFORD

If in a car, park in the facilities for Bradgate Park on the right in the village.

I assume everyone living in or near Leicester is all-too familiar with the park. However, apart from Old John, the ruins and the friendly deer, there are a few features which few people know or recognise.

Follow the footpath along the side of stream, between the ancient pollarded oak trees struggling to survive. Further along the path can be found a substantial boulder known as the Wishing Stone (140:523099). In the 1920s it was reported in the *Leicester Mercury* that 'there are people who still climb it, sit on that rock, meditate, and wish'

Those who have the time and find the park not too crowded can walk over to Old John. On the *far side* of the wall and gate, near the toilet block and car park can be found the standing stone referred to below.

Alternatively, return to the car park and drive around to the car park nearest to Old John, that is by driving through the village, with its range of attractive old houses, then following the road around to the right. The

Postcard of Wishing Stone (pre-1907)

car park entrance finally appears on the right near a road joining on the left.
Without entering the gates into the park itself, enter the woods to the left of the toilet block. About fifty yards in, more or less in the middle of the trees, you should be able to find a substantial standing stone, with a rough ring of smaller recumbent stones mingled around in the bracken (129:524116). When and by who this was erected remains quite unknown.
Take the lane (signed 'Shepshed') heading north-east which is more-or-less opposite the exit to the car park. At the crossroads turn left. Although from this direction it is difficult to see from the road because of the trees, after nearly a mile there is a footpath on the right (opposite the lane leading off left) which runs near the ruins of:
ULVERSCROFT PRIORY.
This is the most complete remains of a monastic house and church in Leicestershire (129:502128). Although nothing earlier than the thirteenth century survives, the Priory was founded in 1134 by the Augustinians. There are two curiosities of folklore - a legend that is haunted by the sound of a sword fight and another which claims there to be an underground tunnel all the way to Leicester Abbey.
Please note these grounds are strictly private and the owners do not welcome casual visitors (although helpful in showing around prearranged groups).

Charnwood Forest geology
The rocks here are the oldest to come to the surface in England, dating back to the Precambrian period - probably between 700 million and 800 million years old. At this time the area was under the sea, with a number of volcanoes throwing ash into the water. After this major earth movements lifted the rocks up into mountains, where the usual processes of erosion reduced their height. By 180 million years ago the climate was hot and dry like parts of the Persian Gulf or American south-west. Heavy rainstorms caused the valleys to be filled with red muddy deposits which dried out for a few years before another storm took place. Where the streams run through Bradgate Park it is still possible to see these deposits washing away as red soil. The Ice Ages caused the region to be covered at least twice, and led to further erosion and alterations to the details of the geological landscape.

Continue heading south-west, going straight over the cross roads, until you reach the B587. Turn right, which will bring you to a small settlement known as:

COPT OAK

St Peter's church (129:483129) has only existed since the 1837. Indeed most of the churches in Charnwood Forest only originated in the nineteenth century. Apart from parishes around the edge of the forest, such as Woodhouse and Groby, the main part of the upland area was all within the one large parish of Whitwick.

However, Copt Oak was an important landmark for centuries. The name 'copt' implies a tree which had been pollarded and indeed an ancient oak tree stood in what is now the churchyard until 1855 when it fell down. At this time it was only 20 feet high but was 24 feet in girth.

Turn right and left over the staggered crossroads and take the B587 over the M1.

The large hill on the left is Bardon Hill, at nearly 1,000 feet the highest point in Leicestershire. Although what little of the summit the quarry company have left is now wooded, there is slight evidence that this was once an iron age hill fort. In the last century there was a picturesque summerhouse on top - alas, those prepared to make the trek to the top will be greeted only by chain link fencing to prevent anyone tumbling down the sheer cliff into the quarry.

Just after the schools turn right at the crossroads. At the staggered crossroads take the left turn which will soon bring you to:

MOUNT ST BERNARD ABBEY

The gateway is conspicuous although has no sign (except 'No entry after 7.30pm')

Rather a curiosity this - although not built until 1837, it was the first monastery in England to be founded after Henry VIII's Dissolution. The austere but impressive buildings are the work of Pugin and represent an early proficiency for the Gothic revival. The attractively laid out walk up and around the Calvary should not be missed.

Return to the road and turn left. Follow in a westerly direction.

Just to the right (east) of the ruined house set back on the skyline is an outcrop known as the Altarstones (129:454169). Indeed, someone has set a large rock across the upstanding crags to form just such a feature. I think its history goes no further than some eighteenth or nineteenth century antiquarian's Druidic fantasies.

Just along to the west is an outcrop known as High Sharpley. This is the remains of the core of a volcano which, many millions of years ago, spewed out the ash and lava which make up some of the rocks of the neighbourhood.

Whitwick Well in 1842

Take the first road to the right (signed 'Shepshed') and pull up almost immediately in the small car park.

The massive outcrop above is Swannimote Rocks and was once the meeting place for the Forest's moot. The exact site is not known, although one area at the top is still relatively flat and this might be the venue.

Turn right from the car park and back to the T-junction. Turn right. Enter the built up area and take the first left just past the Man with Compass pub (Cademan Street)). Turn right at the B587 and (if in a car) turn left soon after the White Horse pub and pull up in the road by the Black Horse pub.

WHITWICK

Pronounced 'wit-ik'. The church by the road is dedicated to St John the Baptist (129:435163). Rather unusually, it is set in a natural amphitheatre and was almost certainly an important pre-christian site, not least because a well still rises steady from underneath the chancel. This is now piped away - the pipe can be seen at the east end of the church wall - and discharges through a spout into the Grace Dieu Brook. I have been reliably informed that in the nineteenth century, long before electricity was usually available to power the blowers on church organs and the task was undertaken by boys, some ingenious person contrived to use the water power from the spring to power the bellows. All evidence of this has now gone.

While at the east end of the church look up on the south wall of the chancel. A small, rather eroded, fragment of interlace is all that survives from an Anglo-Saxon cross shaft which must once have sanctified this place. The church itself is mostly from the fourteenth century but much restored in 1845 and subsequently. The interior has a fourteenth century font and some eroded effigies of this period.

Cross the Grace Dieu Brook and look up at the large mound ahead. This is all that survives of a Norman castle. It would have been more complete if the nineteenth century railway had not cut through - you are probably standing on the place where the tracks ran, and the remains of a platform are just to the right (south-east).

Return to the car, turn around and turn left at the T-junction by the Black Horse (cyclists simply remount and continue along the B587). Follow the B587 north-west (signed Loughborough) through Thringstone. This is roughly following the line of the Grace Dieu Brook. At the A512 turn right. Car drivers should take the next left and pull up in a safe place.

When crossing or walking along the main road be especially careful of the fast traffic. Children and dogs will need careful supervision.

On the south side of the main road is:

GRACE DIEU PRIORY

Strictly, this was not a priory but an Augustinian nunnery, founded in 1240 (129:436183). And what can be seen is not the priory itself but a Tudor house. The ruins are unusually picturesque, not least because they remain rather overgrown and surrounded by fallen masonry, just as most ruins were until 'renovated' in recent decades.

There is a squat mark stone nearly a yard high in the field adjacent to the priory on the west side (129:43401862). It appears to be a conglomerate, commonly referred to as 'pudding stone' or 'breeding stone' (see page 29 for further discussion about conglomerates). This stone leans to the south, a flat side aligns east-west and a notch in the top, possibly man-made, aligns north-south.

A white lady ghost is said to emanate from the stone and cross over the adjacent road, once causing a bus to stop to pick her up at which moment she vanished. An estate worker reported seeing her many times and said 'She was in white and wore a big hat with a wide brim.' The nuns of the Augustinian order wore all-white habits. Legend tells that at the time of the Dissolution the last canoness hid valuable relics before attempting to flee. She was stopped by the King's men and supposedly killed for failing to reveal the hiding place. This tale is supported by the fact that her name was the only one omitted from the pension list for the Priory.

When the property subsequently passed into the hands of the Beaumont family several inexplicable fires destroyed most of the buildings. Another inexplicable event occurred when during a trial on the site a defendant protested his innocence by saying that if he were lying the ground should open up and swallow him - which it immediately did! The judge ruled that this had no bearing on the case and dismissed the charge! Later it was found that old coal seams underlie this area which explains the cause, but not the timing, of this event.

But these are not the only anomalous phenomena of the area. In the last few years a policeman parked nearby saw the figure of a hooded monk on the rear seat of his patrol car.

Return to the A512 and head east. Take the third right turn (at a crossroads) which brings you up the hill with the windmill on (129:462181). Follow this road uphill, across the crossroads. Car drivers should pull up near the track to Lubcloud Farm.

Note: this part of the tour overlaps closely with Tour 9.

Take the bridlepath, following the waymarking through the farmyard (ensuring all gates are left closed). The Grey Hangman Stone, the destination of this short walk, is not on the bridlepath and permission to visit *must* be obtained from the farm. Be warned - this is a working dairy farm and in wet weather suitable waterproof footwear is essential.

Grey Hangman Stone and Ives Head

The bridlepath leads up the hill, through the middle of the field. After the gate at the top leave the path and cross the fence on the left. Keep to the edge of the field and enter the small wood. On the other side of the wood, in the shade of a splendid oak tree (129:47951665) is the:

GREY HANGMAN STONE

A legend associates this fairly modest-sized stone with the accidental hanging of a deer poacher called John of Oxley, but as the stone is too small this may be a corruption of a much older event. Similar legends of poachers strangled by their quarry - typically a sheep - are known from many other places including Staffordshire, Yorkshire and Gloucestershire. It seems probable that such legends are a folk memory of a more complex event, perhaps of ritual sacrifice or mock-sacrifice.

The noticeable oval mound around the base of the stone is said to comprise of stones cleared from the fields. If this is true then the original height of the stone could be up to two feet more than that now visible.

The double-peaked summit of Ives Head is prominent to the north-east. This is the penultimate feature on the ley running through Anstey, described on page 83.

Return to the road the way you came and take the road a short way south-east. Soon after the road joins from the right there is a footpath which leads to the scout camp (in summer months the tents can be clearly seen a few fields away). Cars should be left by the road.

Take the footpath into the trees. Towards the north-west side of the wood you should be able to spot a large standing stone - to my knowledge, the largest one still standing in the county (129:474154). But its close proximity to the Scout camp makes me cautious about attributing any antiquity to it.

Return to the road and continue heading south-east, go under the M1. Cross straight over the B5350. At the B591 left. Head north-east, across the B5330 and up to the car park entrance for:

BEACON HILL

No pretences for this being 'little-known' - but how many visitors realise that the shallow ditches between the car park and the dry-stone wall are the remains of a bronze age hill fort?

It is unusual to find such direct evidence for bronze age earthworks as they are always quite shallow and easily eroded. More particularly, the hill forts created in the bronze age tended to be taken over in the iron age when much more substantial earthworks obliterated the earlier ditches.

The course of the bronze age ditches can be followed to the south-east of the summit, but bracken and undergrowth makes this difficult.

Although archeologists still call these features 'hill forts' we should not assume that their primary function was military. This is especially true of the bronze age when the lifestyle was predominately peaceful and the hill top earthworks too inadequate for defensive purposes. Rather these elevated earthworks were more of tribal centres, perhaps associated with ritual gatherings.

Little archaeological investigation has taken place on Beacon Hill but chance finds reveal that bronze was being melted and cast into tools up here.

One quite a different level of interest, walk around to the western side of the outcrop and crags. When standing towards the south-west and looking north there is one part of the cliff which has acquired the nickname the 'Devil's Face' as it bears more than a passing resemblance to a man's head in profile.

As befits a beacon site, there are superb views. A toposcope has been installed to help identification of distant features. If you happen to be up here around sunset at midsummer then you may be intrigued to observe that the sun descends over the next major hill to the north-west - Breedon on the Hill and its church.

Return to the B591 and turn left, heading east. Descend the hill.

Just past the road to the left is a golf course with a prominent outcrop in the middle. This is known as the Hangingstone Hills, although the perilously perched 'hanging stone' is known to have fallen in 1791.

Turn right at Ye Olde Bull's Head and proceed through Woodhouse Eaves. At the T-junction turn right and then follow left.

I assume most people following this tour will not regard Swithland Woods as 'little-known'. If however you are not local then do stop and enjoy this pretty woodland, especially in spring when the bluebells take over (car park along the lane immediate right at 129:538129). There are several deep, partly-water-filled pits which are the remains of the workings for Swithland slate. These were

Beaumanor Hangingstone
before and after its fall
(after Nichols)

rendered uneconomical when the railways began bringing the thinner Welsh slates to the Midlands.

Within Swithland Wood are several boundary markers comprising pieces of local slate about two feet high with the letter 'S' carved on them. They are not of any great antiquity although I have not established with certainty what the 'S' was an abbreviation for - although I feel fairly sure that they mark the one-time limits of Swithland parish.

Proceed east through the village of:

SWITHLAND

Note the circular lock up about opposite the Griffin Inn. Further on, St Leonard's church (129:555128) is small and attractive. It has thirteenth century origins but has been restored. Rather predictably, there are some early examples of the use of Swithland slate for tombstones. The most artistically adventurous use of slate is on the panels decorating the tomb of Sir John Danvers which depict scenes from the farming year. Note too that it is right on the edge of the churchyard. This is because Sir John decreed that he wanted to be buried with his dog - which could not be allowed in hallowed ground. So, pragmatically, the tomb straddles the churchyard wall.

Just to the east of the church one can stand at a field gate and see in the middle of the field an impressive openwork lantern cross which dates back to around 1500 (129:556126). It originally stood in Mountsorrel, but the eighteenth

94

century owner of Swithland Hall took a fancy to it and decided it would be better where he could see it from his home. In exchange he built the multi-columned and domed 'cross' which still stands in Mountsorrel.

Take the roads heading north-east over the dam of Swithland Reservoir (Great Central Railway steam trains add regular appeal as they run over the viaduct and adjacent embankment). Aim for Mountsorrel (there are two routes which will take you - it is easier to follow the signs or read the map than describe).

MOUNTSORREL

When you reach the B351 (Rothley Road) turn left.

Lanes and tracks lead near the top of Castle Hill (129:577147). Nineteenth century archaeological activities revealed Roman remains, including a fourth century well. The Norman castle site has been removed by quarrying activities.

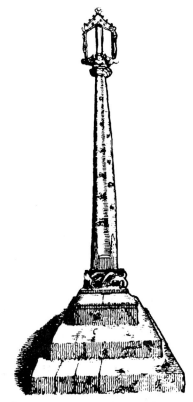

Mountsorrel cross, now in Swithland (from Nichols)

Turn left onto the old main road and follow north.

By the main street can be seen the attractive 'Cross' - although its circular colonnade and roofed shape is anything but cross-like it no doubt offered some shelter to the vendors of butter and other produce at the weekly market. There were once a number of such structures - for instance at Loughborough - but this is one of the few in the Midlands to have survived.

Return south and turn right back onto the B5351 which, after an initial bend, runs due south into:

ROTHLEY

Pronounced 'roeth-lea', the church here can be a mite tricky to find as it is tucked away round the back of the houses at the end of a cul-de-sac (129:586126).

Keep left at the village green then take first right by the junction (Anthony Street). At the Woodman's Stroke pub turn left - you are nearly there!

By the way, the Woodman's Stroke is yet another of the county's pubs which

Anglo-Saxon cross shaft at Rothley (from Nichols)

has attempted to increase its custom by encouraging tales of a ghost.

The church is dedicated to SS Mary and John the Baptist. Apart from a Norman font it has little of any great age - except for a magnificent Anglo-Saxon cross shaft of about the ninth century standing in the churchyard to the south. This is the largest surviving in Leicestershire, although unfortunately without its head. Such an elaborate feature is perhaps to be expected for Rothley as it was the centre of an Anglo-Saxon royal estate.

In the churchyard too is a famous slate commemorating William Hunt who died in 1794 with a carving showing the Last Judgement taking place in Swithland churchyard.

Return along Anthony Street and turn left, then left again into North Street. Take first right (signed Cropston) which is the B5328. Detour into the cul-de-sac to your left by the Blue Bell Inn to take in the picturesque timber framed cruck house and other cottages around the green (129:582123).

Return to the B5328 and turn left. A short way along the B5328 after the village ends you will see the ostentatious gateposts which now lead to the Rothley Court Hotel. Drive in and pull up in the main car park.

You will see a small thirteenth century chapel incorporated into the wing of the house. This was built by the Knights Templar as part of their Preceptory - the red cross on white background associated with these military monks is used on a variety of signs by the hotel management. I have always found the hotel receptionists happy to provide casual visitors with a key, although the interior is not particularly exciting,. The original dedication seems to have been to the local Anglo-Saxon martyr, St Wistan.

Follow the one way system out and turn left, onto the B5328 again. Continue into and through Cropston and turn left onto the B5328 which will return you to Anstey.

Tour 9 North-west Leicestershire

Saxon sculpture and unparalleled places

OS sheets: 128 and 129
Approximately 19 miles

BREEDON ON THE HILL

Few directions are needed to guide visitors to this prominent hill top church (129:406233) apart from noting that the lane to the top is entered from the green to the south of the village.

The name derives from the Celtic for hill, 'bree' (one of the few Celtic place-names surviving in the Midlands), combined with the Old English for hill, 'don' - which translates as 'hill hill on the hill'.

The church, although quite sizeable, is but a small part of the original abbey buildings which grew up on the site of an early seventh or eight century Anglo-Saxon minster (missionary 'mother church'). No doubt a cleric called Hardolf was important to the founders as the church is till dedicated to him and St Mary. Unfortunately nothing else is known of Hardolf.

The hill top was special in earlier times too, being a major iron age hill fort (although most of this is either quarried away or under the present churchyard). Excavation revealed that this was built in two phases. The first was a limestone wall reinforced with timbers. After the timbers decayed a new wall was built in front and the banks stabilised with turf. The rampart and traces of the broad flat-bottomed ditch can be seen on the west and some remnants of the inturned entrance survive on the west side next to and under the churchyard wall. Much pottery and other refuse was found on the site which suggest occupation from the third century BCE to the first century CE.

Although one of the more frequently visited churches in Leicestershire, the treasures of Anglo-Saxon sculpture are quite unjustly little-known, as they are examples of carving without equal in the country. Many are now incorporated in the interior south and east walls although some are high up in the nave and others, such as the angel, in the tower and only accessible by prior arrangement with the churchwardens. There are also fragments of three Anglo-Saxon cross shafts, including one which combines christian imagery with what appears to be a pagan scene depicting the entry of heroes into Valhalla.

The Anglo-Saxon friezes at Breedon are unequalled in quantity, quality and preservation. Some are deeply incised interlace patterns, others are more

97

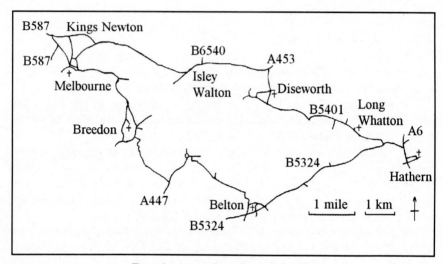

Tour 9 - starts Breedon on the Hill

vine-like. Most of the vines are 'inhabited' with highly stylised or mythical beasts. The skill of carving so deeply such small details is itself impressive; even more astounding is that the animals should appear so

Above and below: *Parts of the Anglo-Saxon friezes from Breedon church* animated as they prance and fight their way across the various scenes.

During the eighth century the Mercian kingdom, under Offa, was at its most powerful and had developed contacts with the Holy Roman Empire and Charlemagne. The exchange of illuminated books, needlework and jewellery led to dramatic changes in artistic style. The Breedon carvings show Northumbrian and Irish influences and from Byzantium, as well as individual designs that may be in the local Mercian tradition. These sculptures are stylistically close to the Lindisfarne Gospels and St Chad's Gospels (from Lichfield), and other examples now in Rome, Paris and Stockholm.

Like these illuminated manuscripts the sculptures were originally brightly coloured and the friezes would probably have formed a continuous decorative band around the minster.

Note that these Anglo-Saxon carvings are not from the first minster church but from a later building of the late eight or early ninth century. The angel is later still, from about 1000.

According to legend, the church was to be built lower down but every night doves carried the newly-laid stones up to the top of the hill. I think that this is perhaps wishful thinking on the part of whichever mere humans were given the arduous task of taking the building stone to the summit!

From later centuries the effigies and large Shirley monument - with cadaver underneath - are of particular interest. Note that the heraldic arms of the Shirley family use a Saracen's head as a crest.

Return to the bottom of the hill and turn left. From Breedon take the lane south-east. This is tricky to spot - when you see the newsagents on the left you are almost there. The subtle sign to Osgathorpe will confirm the turn. (If you miss it, turn around in the quarry entrance which soon comes up on the left.) The lane is rather twisting but eventually leads to a give way. Turn left onto the A447 and turn right at the roundabout. Take the immediate right, then after nearly a mile turn right at the give way to take the lane that descends to:

BELTON

Turn left in the village before the Queens Head and pull up by the church and The George pub.

You are by the only permanent maypole in Leicestershire (129:3448208), splendidly painted in three bands of red, white and blue and surmounted by a fox weather vane. Some may think this to be a typical Leicestershire image, but permanent maypoles throughout the country tend to have weathervanes with either the ubiquitous cock or a fox.

Up on a mound and overlooking the open area is the tower and spire of St John the Baptist's church. A mostly fourteenth century church, although the font is a century older. There are angels on the stone corbels in the nave and curious carvings around the south capital of the chancel arch. The table top tomb has an effigy of the founder of Grace Dieu nunnery, Lady Roesia de Verdun.

Continue to the left of the church to the give way and turn left to take the B5324 north-east (notice the twin-horned aspect of Ives Head on the Charnwood Forest skyline to the right - a standing stone just the other side is visited on Tour 8). Turn right on the A6 then by the 40 mph speed restriction and the Jet petrol station turn left into Wide Lane. Continue to the church and turn right before pulling up.

HATHERN

SS Peter and Paul (129:503224) has a late Anglo-Saxon or early Norman font and a fragment of Anglo-Saxon cross shaft. In the churchyard are numerous excellent slate headstones.

At the end of this road, in the centre of the old village (129:503223) is a fine cross with an octagonal moulded capital probably form the fourteenth century. The shaft was replaced in the early 1920s after a gale in January 1916

Hathern cross. Left: In the 17902 (from Nichols). *Right:* In early 1990s

demolished the original. It is possible that the original was weakened by the practice of lighting bonfires on the top. This was common around the turn of the century and the end of the Boer War was celebrated by burning an effigy of General Kruger on there.

Retrace your route back up the A6 and left onto the B5324 but take the first right into:

LONG WHATTON

The fourteenth century church of All Saints (129:483233) was rebuilt in 1866. The tower ended up in an unusual position and the west front has imposing triple gables. There are two medieval moats to the north of the church, both now dry, although one has been excavated in recent years.

Continue through the village, noticing the various timber-framed and thatched houses, with decorative figures such as foxes made from thatch and placed on the ridge. Towards the north-west end of the village, in the yard of Uplands Farm, is a well-preserved rag-and-chain pump. This method of raising water was particularly efficient.

Passing under the M1 and over the A42, the B5401 leads into:

DISEWORTH

101

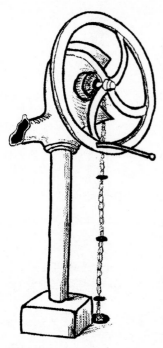

Take the first right and pull up near the crossroads with the Bull and Swan pub (once two separate but adjacent hostelries). This part of the village is known as The Cross but, if there ever was such a structure, no evidence survives.

Pronounced 'dyes-worth' the village retains a clear sense of having been planned around a central crossroads. The church of St Michael and All Angels sits on a mound to the south-east (129:454245). The church is mostly thirteenth century but there is one Norman window in the chancel. To the south-west in Hall Gate is a prominent timber-framed house which was the birthplace of William Lilly (born 1602) who became the favourite astrologer of Charles I.

The street-names intrigue me: Lady Gate, Hall Gate, Clement Gate and Grimes Gate. The 'gate' is clearly local Scandinavian-influenced dialect for 'road' or 'path'. Bear in mind that the pagan metalworking deity, Wayland the Smith, was commonly christianised as St Clement, and that Grimr was a common nickname for the god Odin or Woden (as in Wednesday), perhaps we should also look upon 'lady' as a literal translation of the name of the goddess Freya (who is still honoured in Friday). If so, is Hall Gate the road to the manorial hall, or the corruption of the Old English word *halig*, which gives us 'holy'? We will never know, but the whole notion of villages and towns being built around a sacred centre - such as crossroads - is worldwide and quickly becomes a complex topic. I have presented some further ideas in my booklet *The quest for the omphalos - finding the mystical middle of England* (Heart of Albion Press 1991; now out of print).

Long Whatton chain pump.

While this book is intended to promote the best of Leicestershire and Rutland, anyone who has travelled any distance should cross over into south Derbyshire and visit one of the finest Norman churches in the region.

Take Grimes Gate north and turn left at the A453. Continue, ignoring the major turn to Castle Donington. In Isley Walton notice the curious cottages beside the road and turn immediate right. Follow to the next settlement and turn right immediately after the bridge by the 30 mph speed restriction. This is:
KINGS NEWTON

A few hundred yards along, on the right, is a modern cross. The inscription commemorates an event which never happened - the coronation of Edward VIII (128:391262). The village is a show-piece of well-restored old buildings. Pull up near Ye Olde Packe Horse pub and look to the north side of the road for a footpath sign which also points to the 'holy well'. This is fairly easy to find, nestling in a tree-shaded dell (128:385263).

At the cross roads by this pub take the street heading south (signed 'Melbourne') to a triangular green, Turn left. Immediately turn right at a second triangular green. Pull up. You are now in:

MELBOURNE

The small stone structure on the green is the Lily Well (128:387255).

Continue along Castle Street and keep left at the large open space with car parking in the centre. Pull up by the substantial stone wall on the left.

The private garden behind this wall of Castle Farm contains the remains of substantial stone foundations for the castle built in 1311 (although nothing is visible from the street).

Continue to the church ahead; car drivers park where convenient.

A tea shop and craft shops can be found if desired. However, the main attraction is the splendours of St Mary's, an almost complete Norman church (128:389250). Keep an eye out for carved capitals - the south entrance doorway has one of a falling or drowning man clutching what I take to be his purse or money bag.

Inside, try to imagine the upper floor which once spanned the nave, providing a two-story interior. The crossing under the tower has some of the finest carvings, including a female exhibitionist or 'sheela-na-gig' and various animated animals.

Why was such a large church erected here? It seems that the Bishop of Carlisle found his home region rather troubled with invaders from north of the border so he retreated to the safety of the Trent valley. We have here then, to all intents and purposes, a twelfth century episcopal church.

Do not leave without walking down to the lake and enjoying the attractive landscaping.

From the church's car park turn right (east) and follow the lane leading to the hamlet of Wilson. Follow the lane through which will bring you back to Breedon.

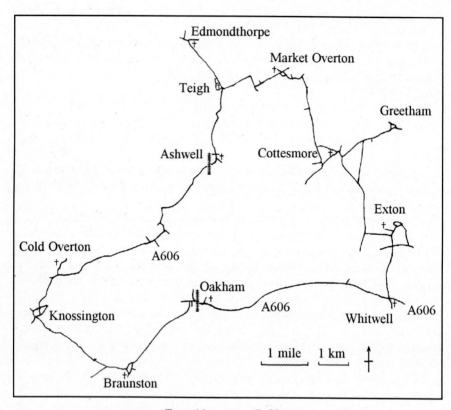

Tour 10 - starts Oakham

Tour 10 North Rutland
'Queens' and wells

OS sheets: 130 and 141
Approximately 29 miles

OAKHAM
Oakham retains a wide range of buildings of historical interest such as the substantial polygonal timber market cross. Even the stocks have the peculiarity of five holes. Was this for contortionists or just a spare for a regularly-offending one-legged man? No doubt other even worse suggestions have been put forward too.

Another building well worth a visit is the church of All Saints (141:861089). Much of the building can be dated to the fourteenth century. There are many exterior carvings and fine carved capitals inside. The capital nearest the pulpit has a Green Man, while over the pulpit is a tongue-poking girner. Other capitals include a dragon and the tale of the fox and the geese.

On the outside look for two girning gargoyles on north of the tower. While looking up, the weather vane, known as Cock Peter, is one of the oldest in England, perhaps dating to the fourteenth century.

The nearby Castle, still showing clearly its origins as a Norman Great Hall, has various Norman carvings of animals and paired heads among the better-known collection of ornamental horseshoes. Some eroded and enigmatic figures are set in the exterior wall. Oakham Great Hall is the earliest surviving hall of any English castle, dating to 1180-90.

Our Lady's Well at Oakham was once famed for curing sore eyes providing that a pin was thrown in first. In 1291 indulgences could be obtained by visiting Oakham Church during its patronal festival - All Saints - and there was a pilgrimage (at a price) to Our Lady's Well. In 1881 it was visited by the future Queen Alexandra. However, it is now in an area of neglected ground beside a housing estate off the B668 to Cottesmore (141:866095).

Leave Oakham by the west. Immediately after the level crossing turn left and take the second left to:
BRAUNSTON
In the village turn left at the Old Plough (unless you want to stop and enjoy the excellent food and beers). Continue around to the church. (141:833066).

Another All Saints but of quite different character. The tower and clerestory are again fourteenth century. Apart from a Norman font, doorway and chancel arch, plus traces of fifteenth century wall paintings the main interest for most people will be the so-called 'Earth Mother' carving which now stands to the west of the tower. She - of that there can be no doubt - is of a unique style without parallel. The carving was at some time buried face down and used as a doorway threshold. Early this century repair work led to her being rediscovered. Some have suggested she is a rare example of Anglo-Saxon - or even Iron Age - stone carving, but there is no evidence to support this and a fourteenth century date is more probable.

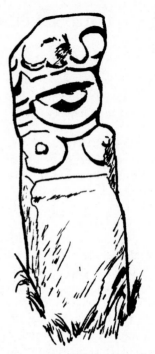

Braunston 'Earth Mother'

The church stands on a slight mound within the once-circular churchyard. The nearby River Gwash was once the boundary between Leicestershire and Rutland. It is quite probable that Braunston was a significant pre-christian Anglo-Saxon settlement with the Leighfield Forest. But when and where the carving fits in to all this is quite unclear.

In the churchyard look for two slates, carved in 1787 and 1795, which depict the Resurrectioñ.

Leave Braunston by the west and then take the minor lane on the right to Knossington. Head for the north and into:

COLD OVERTON

If there is one church in Leicestershire and Rutland which offers the greatest variety of figurative carvings, it has to be St John the Baptist's at Cold Overton (130:810102). Every conceivable - and several inconceivable - parts of the fabric have been adorned with heads and grotesques. It brings to mind some medieval mason pondering on the philosophical debate about how many angels could dance on the head of a pin and deciding he would find out how many could be accommodated on one church. Except, quite clearly, it is not the work of one lifetime but rather an onğoing tradition that reconciles both the most naive faces that seem like little more than pebbles with scratches for eyes and mouth through to several sculptural *tour de force* of characterisation.

106

Carving on Cold Overton church tower

Inside the porch are various heads, some in wood others in stone. In the nave are fine corbel heads - that in the south-east corner is griffin-like and in the north-east is a beaked head. In the chancel is a blocked north door to the vestry which has two plain but clearly asymmetrical faces on the corbels; opposite is a sedilia with three similarly quirky faces. . Additional splendours include the twelfth century glass in the south chancel window and wall paintings in the south aisle.

On the exterior north chancel wall are two unusual heads, one with hare-like ears and the other stylised with two holes for eyes and what might be intended to be a beak. Also look at the base of the tower and the pinnacles above the south aisle for further faces.

Just for fun, look out for the ironstone used to construct the porch which contains several well preserved fossils of brachipods (shellfish) and belemnites (slate-pencil shaped cuttlefish 'bones'). And don't miss the scratch dial or the fine yew trees.

Return to the the road which leads east to Langham. Turn right at the A606 and then turn left at the first bend. Further into the village turn left, following the sign to:

ASHWELL

At the level crossing car drivers will need to follow directions to raise the barriers. Stop by the T-junction.

In a small glade of trees is the well which gives the village its name (130:874137). Although these days known as the Wishing Well, earlier documents make it clear that it was considered to be a holy well.

An inscription above the well reads:

All ye who hither come to drink,
Rest not your thoughts below,
Look at that sacred sign and think
Whence living waters flow.

The inscription has lost its nub, as the cross which stood over the well is now in private hands.

Turn left at the T junction and pull up by the next right turn.

Ashwell

The church (130:866137) was heavily restored in 1851, when the churchyard cross was erected, but there are traces of the fourteenth century structure and a Norman arch. A wooden effigy of a knight, which dates to the fourteenth century, is only of only two in the county. Keeping him company is an incised marble slab which is fifteenth century. In the vestry to the north of the chancel is another marble effigy.

Head north from Ashwell into:
TEIGH
Pronounced 'tea' or 'tee' this is one of thirty-one 'Thankful Villages' - that is, all those who served in World War I came back (eleven men and two women).
Turn left to the take the road which loops in a semi-circle around the churchyard of Holy Trinity (130:865160).
This has a thirteenth century tower although the rest dates to 1782. There is no exterior figurative carving. Inside is a curious pulpit which stands thirteen feet above ground. The oak screen in the tower arch has a painting of a leaded window.
Rejoin the road heading north and turn right in:
EDMONDTHORPE
St Michael's (130:857176) is fourteenth century, with a fifteenth century screen. The massive three-decker monument is to the local Smith family

depicting two wives and of one husband. One wife is carved in Derbyshire alabaster and curious markings on her wrist have led to a folklore of her being involved in witchcraft. The tale goes that she could transform herself into a cat. One day a servant in the household got annoyed with the cat's antics and hit out at it with a cleaver, injuring a paw. Soon after the wife of the household was found in bed, suffering from injuries to her wrist. The crack and red stain on her monument are held as evidence for the unlikely truth of this tale.

Two other monuments are also curious. In the chancel is a strange affair, with a Hebrew motto and incomplete inscription. This has no dates of death so was obviously completed in time for the persons commemorated to admire the way they would be seen by posterity. Note that the superstitious letter carver stopped short of stating they 'dyed'.

In the north aisle is a more ordinary memorial tablet - until you notice that the person's name was William Ann Pochin. One wonders what family tradition was being maintained with this highly unusual - at least for a man - middle name.

The chancel arch is ornamented with a pair of corbels - the southern one has a singularly disturbing grimace.

There is old graffiti in the porch. Although not accessible, on the lead roof there are shoe outlines and initials with dates from the mid-1700s to 1978. These probably are the mementoes of workmen doing repairs.

Also on the outside is a 'full circle' scratch dial.

Further along the village street (outside the old school, now a social centre) is a distinctive Victorian cast iron pump in the shape of a dragon.

Return to Teigh and turn left to:
MARKET OVERTON
The church of SS Peter and Paul (130:885165) stands on the scarp of a hill overlooking the Vale of Catmose. It is also the site of a Roman camp and an Anglo-Saxon cemetery. In the base of the tower are incorporated substantial fragments of two Anglo-Saxon cross shafts. The churchyard stile in the north-west corner also incorporates Anglo-Saxon columns. Inside the church is an Anglo-Saxon tower arch - the 'only worthwhile piece of Anglo-Saxon architecture in the county' according to Pevsner. Of a much later date are the faces in the arch springers.

Despite all these early traces, do not miss the early fourteenth century doorway and ironwork. The sundial on the tower was reputedly given by Sir Isaac Newton; it is known that his mother was from Market Overton.

The field to the east of the church was used for fairs until quite recent times. The Black Bull Inn opposite has a well-deserved reputation which brings in customers from a wide area.

Turn right by the Black Bull.
Note the stocks and whipping post on the green opposite the Three Horseshoes

Follow this road then turn left in:

COTTESMORE

St Nicholas (130:903136) has a Norman south doorway in an otherwise fourteenth and fifteenth century church. The fourteenth century font stands on an older base. The pulpit is Jacobean.

Continue north-east along the B668 to:

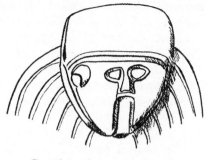

Greetham font tongue-poker

GREETHAM

Take the third left in the village (Church Lane) which will bring you to St Mary's church (130:924146).

There are several dozen small heads around the nave and tower roofs - some with a rather demonic aspect. Inside, there is part of an Anglo-Saxon cross in the inside west wall of the south aisle. Fragments of Norman tympanum are in the south aisle west wall. But the most splendid treasure is the font, which dates to about 1200. There are four heads forming corner crockets - one monster, two animals and the other human with an elongated tongue.

Continue back to the B668 and on your right at the road junction is:

Greetham well (130:925145). Although a substantial and well-cared for structure it has always looked dry when visited. The cistern at the back suggests the flow has always been meagre or erratic or possibly that the structure is a 'fake' fed by piped water.

On one stone is an inscription similar to that at Ashwell:

All ye who hither come to drink
rest not your thoughts below
remember Jacob's Well and think
whence living waters flow.

Greetham well

110

Return towards Cottesmore. Ignore the farm access then turn left. At the give way turn left, then continue past the nursery entrance and take the next left (at the turning look back over your left shoulder to see the fine gateway surmounted with the famous pair of stags). This will bring you to:

EXTON

On the left, prominently signed, is a track that will bring you to another church dedicated to SS Peter and Paul (141:920112).

One of the finest churches in Rutland, it was restored in 1850. Inside are a number of monuments from the fourteenth to eighteenth centuries displaying a range of taste and ostentation. Some of these include the 'fruity' carvings of Gibbons. The font is fourteenth century and has unusually prominent heads above a more characteristic arcade.

The ruins of an Elizabethan house survive near the church.

Return along the track and turn left.

Proceed into the village where a well house with eight pillars and Colleyweston stone roof stands near the school. It is known as Hawkswell Spring. The sycamore-shaded green to the south is surrounded by stone cottages.

Loop around the village and return past the track to the church.

Pick up the lane running due south to:

WHITWELL

The small church of St Michael (141:924087) stands above a massive retaining wall near a small hill top. The building is basically thirteenth century, including the bellcote, and some fourteenth century stained glass of the crucifixion survives. The font has been dated to about 1200 and is decorated with a wheel and other motifs.

Two subtle features make St Michael's of especial interest. A spring, which rises higher the slope, flows under the chancel. I am reliably informed that after heavy rain the water can be heard running. It now issues from a spout at the side of the main road. The village name derives from 'white well', strongly suggesting a pre-christian sacred site. Documentary evidence suggests that Whitwell provided holy water and sacrificial bread for many other churches in the area.

Allowing for the effects of a hill to the east, St Michael's is the only church in Rutland to align with sunrise on the patronal saint's feast day. This has led me to speculate elsewhere that there is a deliberate alignment between the churches at Oakham, Whitwell and Great Casterton - which is also the axis of Whitwell church.

A major iron age and Roman settlement has been excavated just to the south of the present village, on the shoreline of Rutland Water.

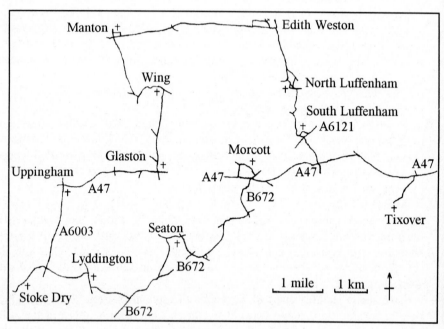

Tour 11 - Starts Lyddington

Tour 11 South Rutland

A maze and many amazing carvings

OS sheet: 141
Approximately 30 miles

LYDDINGTON

The village has a long, attractive Main Street of ironstone-built houses. The Old White Hart provides excellent food and beer in convivial surroundings. If you do not find this all-too pleasurable then walk across the village green, past the remains of the medieval cross (141:875971). It is reduced to a stump about a yard high on a square base. The shaft has four sides with two flutes on each face.

Continue walking towards St Andrew's church (141:877970), which will entail walking through the well-known Bede House - the only English Heritage site in Rutland and, indeed, there are only two more in Leicestershire. The Bede House was built in the late fifteenth century by Bishop Russell and was converted in the sixteenth century into an almshouse.

Inside the church the chancel is fourteenth century and includes an early experiment in acoustics - earthenware jars set into the walls. The rest of the church is mostly fifteenth century, including most of the animal and human grotesques in the nave and aisles. However those at chancel end date only to 1991 and depict on one side the bishop and on the other, maintaining a long tradition, a foliate head. Traces of wall paintings survive. Outside, there are girning gargoyles on the tower.

Take the lane west (Stoke Road) and cross the A6003. Pull up by the church in:

Lyddington cross shaft

STOKE DRY

This is St Andrew's (141:856967), sitting pertly on a mound on the slope above Eyebrook Reservoir. There are two scratch dials on the south side but the real interest is inside.

Although the wooden rood screen is of interest in its own right, it has to be the Norman columns each side which will

113

take your attention. They are densely crammed with strange animals and humans including a bell ringer (this must be one of the earliest depictions of such activities), mermaid and dragon. In the chancel is a Norman string course with tendrils, animals and humans. Apart from the obvious Norman carvings, much of the church dates to about 1300.

There are various effigies. In the side chapel are also quite well-preserved wall paintings. The most prominent is of the martyrdom of the Anglo-Saxon king, St Edmund, by the pagan vikings. These are depicted looking for all the world as Red Indians, this is perhaps less surprising when it is realised that it may have been painted about 1574, soon after the discovery of the New World, and the best-known pagans of the period were indeed New World Indians.

Return to the A6003 and turn left into:

UPPINGHAM

Depending on timing and inclination, the tea shop by the cross roads in the centre of the town may be welcome, or the various craft shops and galleries may appeal more. Otherwise proceed directly to the church of SS Peter and Paul (141:866996). A drastic restoration of 1861 means that the thirteenth and fourteenth century structure is less interesting than it might otherwise be. The only important survivals of the Norman church are four demi-figures which include Christ and a saint giving a blessing. Both are bearded and date to about 1200.

Take the A47 east to:

GLASTON

Turn left at the Monkton Arms and pull up by the churchyard.

St Andrew's has a central tower with a rather short spire (141:896005)

There is twelfth century arcade and a thirteenth century sedilia. Also of that century is a marble coffin. From the fourteenth century is the monument. An Anglo-Saxon cemetery was discovered in a sandpit opposite the church.

Follow the lane north to:

WING

Just coming in to the village pull up by the circular white fence (141:896028).

This is one of only eight surviving medieval turf mazes in Britain (although over thirty others are known but now lost). It is fifty feet across and the same design as that in Chartres cathedral and another turf maze at Alkborough, South Humberside.

Turn left at the T-junction.

Wing maze in about 1850

114

The church of SS Peter and Paul (141:894029) has a Norman south arcade dating to about 1150 and a north arcade and chancel arch of later in the twelfth century. It was rebuilt in 1875.

Leave the village to the west and follow right and right again towards:

MANTON

Turn right at the crossroads then first left at a triangular green, into Stocks Hill.

St Mary's (141:881047) is a Norman church rebuilt in the fourteenth century, except for the tower which is the original Norman fabric now surmounted by a cumbersome bellcote. The font is also Norman. There are small heads in the nave arch springers and two fine corbels at the east end of the chancel, the north-east one girning. Also of note is a medieval stone coffin with a graceful cross. In the churchyard are splendid limestone gravestones.

Take the road east to:

EDITH WESTON

Turn left at The Wheatsheaf (this turn is only visible when nearly there; car drivers should indicate left soon after the 'Edith Weston' name sign on the left hand verge).

The base of a medieval cross survives in the middle of the village (141:927053).

St Mary's (141:927054) has twelfth century origins as the Norman carving on the chancel and north arcade reveals. The tower and attractive spire are fifteenth century. There are bold bug-eyed gargoyles on the corners of the tower.

Take the lane south-east to:

NORTH LUFFENHAM

On the way into the village you pass near to the site of large Anglo-Saxon cemetery with burials dating from about 450 to 650.

Turn right at the edge of the village and left at the Fox and Hounds. The church is on the right of the street, signposted.

St John the Baptist's (141:934033) is mostly thirteenth century, including the wall painting. There is plenty of fourteenth century glass - the main exception is the east window. In the nave roof are wooden angels. Underneath are carved corbels, with one girning and another tongue-poking on the north side. On the south side of the nave are several lively arch springers including a man with his hands over his ears.

Follow through this delightful limestone village and take the minor lane south, signed to:

SOUTH LUFFENHAM

The church is tricky to locate from this direction but is situated in the centre of the narrow streets which make up this intriguing village.

The fourteenth century tower of St Mary's (141:941019) is surmounted by a curiously crocketed spire. The chancel and south arcade are thirteenth century but the rest fourteenth and fifteenth century. In the north aisle arcade are interesting heads including a hare and moustached man. The corbel on the east side of the chancel arch is most odd. The tower features prominent gargoyles.

Cross the A6121 and take the lane south (signed to Barrowden) to the A47. Turn left and take the second right for arguably the most obscure of all the little-known sites:

TIXOVER

Take the lane into the hamlet and pull up by the sign to obtain the key for the church. Continue on through the farm yard and out into the field track the other side. On the left is a grass track down to the church. If driving think twice before proceeding when the ground is muddy!

The church is at least a quarter of a mile from the nearest house, down in a loop of the Welland valley, looking over into Northamptonshire (141:971998). It is dedicated to the much-maligned St Mary Magdalene and contains a Norman font and a thirteenth century arcade plus some effigies and some ancient glass from continental Europe. The tower is mostly Norman with a fifteenth century parapet. On the west side of the tower is an interesting gargoyle.

Return to the A47 and turn left. Follow, not missing the prominent and well-restored windmill into:

MORCOTT

Turn right onto the A6121 then immediate left at the White Horse Inn. The church soon appears on the right, set amidst attractive limestone houses.

St Mary's (141:924007) has, I have established in the course of several visits, frustratingly difficult arrangements for obtaining the key. However, perseverance is well-rewarded as this is the most complete Norman architecture to be seen in Rutland, including a complete Norman arcade with capitals that include animal carvings. The south doorway and the lower parts of the tower are also Norman. The tower arch has

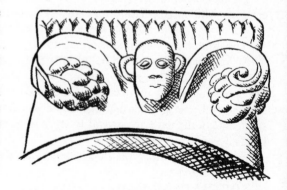

Norman capital in Morcott church with man's head and what are probably intended to be fir cones but may be grapes.

116

serpents carved around the capitals. The circular window in the tower is considered by some to have been reused from an earlier Anglo-Saxon building.

The chancel was rebuilt in the fifteenth century but retains a thirteenth century arch and a fourteenth century tomb. The beautifully carved pulpit is Jacobean.

Take the B672 south from Morcott. Follow around the bends.

On the left appears the towering brick-built viaduct with eighty-two arches each seventy feet high.

Go underneath then turn right and right again into:

SEATON

Turn left and pull up by the George and Dragon (recommended if your conclusion to this tour coincides with opening hours).

All Hallow's church (141:904983) has a late Norman doorway with defaced heads. The chancel arch and arcades are also twelfth century. The tower and spire are fourteenth century. Medieval tombstones are mounted on the outer walls and an ancient font converted to a seat.

Return by a minor lane leading south to rejoin the B672 and then turn first right to return to Lyddington.

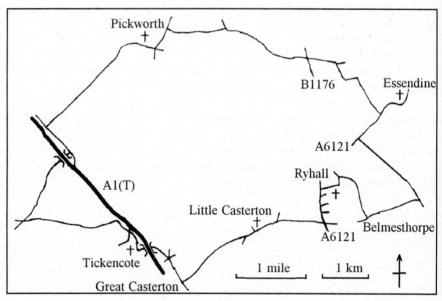

Tour 12 - starts Tickencote

118

Tour 12 East Rutland

Last but not least

OS sheets: 130 and 141
Approximately 16 miles

TICKENCOTE

Tucked in the lee of the fearsomely busy A1 is a unique curiosity. The best way of describing St Peter's church (141:990095) might be 'Normanesque'. There are some beautiful remnants of an important Norman building, but they were restored in 1792, which was long before the subtleties of Norman architecture had been grasped. So, there is a west front inspired by the work of the eighteenth century architect Hawksmoor, a mock-Norman nave and a more-faithfully restored chancel. This is fortunate, as the stone roof vaulting in the chancel has only one parallel in the country, and that is the choir of Canterbury cathedral.

There are numerous faces to be found on corbels, stone roof bosses and even the font (which dates to around 1200). The greatest number are in the five bands of carving around the chancel arch - which over the years has acquired a singularly flattened shape. Beaked heads, Green Men, tongue pokers and girning faces are all there to be found. Perhaps my favourite here is the triple headed central boss on the chancel vault which seems to depict a monk and two muzzled bears.

In the chancel, tucked into the south wall is one of only two wooden effigies in Leicestershire and Rutland (the other is at Ashwell). It dates to the fourteenth century and he has a dog at his feet.

The present altar stands on a block of Purbeck marble that was probably the original 'mensa' or stone altar. In the nave are twelve large and deeply-carved heads, two of which are tongue-pokers. On the outside of the nave, on the south side, is a girning face.

Pass under the A1 and enter:
GREAT CASTERTON
Take the first left in the village (signed Ryhall and Essendine) and pull up about 200 yards along.

On the right hand side of the road are the deep ditches which are the remains of a Roman military camp - clearly relating to troop movements along Ermine Street, then and now the Great North Road (141:002092).

Return to the village and turn left, back onto th~ B1081 (which was the original Great North Road before the dual carriageway bypassed the village).

The church of SS Peter and Paul (141:002088) is said to be on the site of a Roman temple. Whatever the truth of this, there is a Norman font, although most of the church is from the thirteenth century, including three early effigies of that century. One is a full-length figure in good condition and now situated in the south aisle. The other two are older 'blanket effigies' where only the head and feet are depicted. One is under the tower and the other on the outside of the south aisle.

A small tongue poker can be found in the springer of a south aisle arch. Outside, there is a girning gargoyle on the south aisle. Slates in the churchyard include such unusual subjects as the resurrection and the sacrifice of Isaac.

As noted in Tour 10, this church may be the terminus of a short alignment featuring Whitwell church.

Continue along the B1081 a short way and take the first left, the lane north-east to:

LITTLE CASTERTON

Pull up by the minor lane, first left in the village, leading to the footpath which will take you to the small church of All Saints, tucked down by the River Gwash (141:018099).

The Normans were here too and their legacy is a simple, indeed rather crudely carved, tympanum which has a prominent Tree of Life combined with two triple rosettes.

The structure is mostly thirteenth and fourteenth century. From the earlier century survive wall paintings in the jambs of the windows. From the fourteenth century is the piscina canopy with heads, some stained glass and a fine brass memorial in the chancel. There is also a chancel screen, of which the lower half is Tudor, and a collection of angels in the roof.

Follow the lane north-east and turn left at the A6121. Enter:

RYHALL

In the village take fourth road on the right (New Road) which will lead you to the Green Dragon Inn with the church behind (130:036108).

Little Casteron tympanum

120

This inn is on the site of a thirteenth century manor house although only the cellar contains evidence of this.

St John the Evangelist is one of the most ornately decorated churches in the area. The thirteenth century tower and spire, chancel arch and nave arch are adorned with plentiful heads such as the external frieze which includes a green animal on the north aisle and lots of girning heads plus a tongue poker. A Green Man resides over the priest's door; adjoining is a sword-wielding grotesque. See if you can find the bum-poker. All are first class and very varied in style.

The seventh century saint, St Tibba, had a cell on the site of the present church. She was a niece of King Penda, the last of the pagan Mercian kings. In her youth she was a wild, hunting girl but later became a hermit. Although buried in Ryhall her bones were transferred in 936 to Peterborough. A tradition which is still kept alive in the village is that she used to walk up the hill to wash at the spring which bore her name. Over the years this was corrupted to Tibbs's Well Hill and then Stibbalswell Hill. On the brow of the hill is Halegreen which derives from a Saxon word meaning 'gathering to honour saints'. Such meetings were held on St Tibba's Day, 14th December.

Another Anglo-Saxon saint, who was St Tibba's cousin, in a contorted way gives her name to Stableford Bridge (130:036110). Stableford is a contraction of 'St Ebba's well ford'. St Ebba's Well was later known as Shepherd Jacob's Well, but is now lost.

Head north from the church, along Bridge Street, cross the Gwash and turn right. Just to the south-east of Ryhall is:

BELMESTHORPE

The renown Blue Bell pub is on the right.

Turn left at the T-junction in the village.

Almost out of the village, on the left hand side, is a stone-built dovecote. The nesting boxes are visible inside.

Follow the lane, turn left and turn right at the A6121 into:

ESSENDINE

Continue through the village. On the far side, towards the bottom of the hill and just past a row of bungalows on the left (but poorly visible from the road) is St Mary's church (130:049128).

The church has an excellent late Anglo-Saxon or early Norman doorway and chancel arch. The south doorway has a tympanum of Christ in majesty within a vesica pisca and two angels - more typical of the French Norman style. The doorjambs are also carved - what may be Adam and Eve under a tree, a stag under a tree and two men with crooks.

Near the church the main road passes over a a seventeenth century three-arch bridge. Also in the village is the remains of a moated Elizabethan house.

Return up the hill, back over the railway bridge then take the immediate right (signed Pickworth). Follow to the T junction, then turn left, straight over the B1176 crossroads. Follow then take the first left into the woodland.

Although hidden from the road, on the right are earthworks known as Castle Dike (130:008143).

Turn left into:

PICKWORTH

Turn right in the village.

The original fourteenth century church was ruined in the Wars of the Roses and only one arch survives to the west of All Saint's (130:992138), which was built in 1821.

Follow the lane which will lead south-west to the A1. Turn left and turn right for the underpass.

On your right is Bloody Oaks Wood which takes its name from one of the battles of the Wars of the Roses fought on 12th May 1470, known as the Battle of Loosecoat Field. The Lancastrians were defeated and it is said that those on the losing side escaped by taking off their coats which bore identifying colours. The field name is, however, more likely to derive from the Old English *hlose-cot* which means 'pigsty cottage'. The dead from the battle were buried near the old church in Pickworth, as a mass grave was discovered there in the 1970s.

From here follow the lane south-west then turn left at the crossroads. This lane returns to Tickencote.

Notes

Chapter 1
An introduction to holy wells

1: J.C. Cooper cited in Paul Devereux *Earthmind* Harper and Row 1989
2: Paul Devereux *ibid.*
3: Cited in Richard Morris *Churches in the landscape* Dent 1989
4: R. Merrifield *The archaeology of ritual and magic* Batsford 1987
5: See Barrie Cox 'The place-names of Rutland' English Place-Name Society 1994 p199 and 299
6: Since publishing my *Holy wells and springs of Leicestershire and Rutland* in 1990 there has been an independent attempt to survey this subject. James Rattue, 'An inventory of ancient, holy and healing wells in Leicestershire' (*Transactions of the Leicestershire Archaeological and Historical Society* Vol.LXVII 1993 p59-69) lists old and named wells. Regrettably, although adding a few additional sites, he perpetrates some of the errors I made in compiling my previously-published list and appears to have made no effort to follow up with field work.

Chapter two
An introduction to ancient crosses

1: John Michell *The old stones of Land's End* Garnstone 1974
2: J. Irwin 'Pillar and cross' *R.I.L.K.O. newsletter* No.33 pp5-24 1988
3: Derek Bryce *Symbolism of the Celtic cross* Llanerch 1989

Chapter three
An introduction to standing stones and mark stones

1: E. Eisenberg *The Derbyshire year* J.H. Hall and Sons 1989.
2: Full details of parish boundary research can be found in A. Winchester *Discovering parish boundaries* Shire 1990.
3: Cited in W. Johnson *Folk memory* Clarendon 1908.
4: Cited in R. Morris *Churches in the landscape* Dent 1989
5: Cited in Morris *ibid.*
6: Marie-Louise von Franz 'The process of individuation' in C.G. Jung (ed.) *Man and his symbols* Aldus 1964
7: John Michell *The old stones of Land's End* Garnstone 1989
8: Paul Devereux 'The forgotten heart of Albion Part 2' in *The Ley Hunter* No.68 1975 pp9-12; Paul Devereux and Andrew York 'Portrait of a fault

area Part 1' in *The News* No.11 1975 (now *Fortean Times*) and 'Portrait of a fault area Part 2' in *The News* No.12 1976.

Chapter four
An introduction to medieval church carvings

1: N. Pevsner *Leicestershire and Rutland* Penguin 1960

2: National Association of Decorative and Fine Arts Societies *Inside churches* Capability Publishing 1989

3: R. Morris *Churches in the landscape* Dent 1989

4: R.N. Bailey *The meaning of Mercian sculpture* University of Leicester 1990

5: J.H. Vaux 'The Canterbury monsters' Mereborough Books 1989

6: M.A. Murray *The witch-cult in western Europe* Oxford U.P. 1921; for a more up-to-date and reliable treatment see Ronald Hutton *The pagan religions of the ancient British Isles* Blackwell 1991

7: L. Stone *Sculpture in Britain: the middle ages* Penguin 1955

8: R. Sheridan and A. Ross *Grotesques and gargoyles* David and Charles 1975; and G.R. Phillips *The unpolluted god* Northern Lights 1987.

9: Roy Judge *The Jack in the Green* D.B. Brewer for Folklore Society 1979. My thanks to Ronald Hutton for bringing Brewer's work to my attention.

10: K. Basford *The green man* Brewer 1978; W. Anderson *The green man* Harper Collins 1990 which was closely linked to a BBC1 TV programme of the same name in November 1990.

11: G.R. Phillips *The unpolluted god* Northern lights 1987.

12: The first to make this suggestion seems to be the otherwise staid (even prudish) M.D. Anderson in *History and imagery in British churches* John Murray 1971. However for a full survey of sexual images in medieval church carving see Anthony Weir and James Jarman *Images of lust* Batsford 1986.

13: R.N. Trubshaw *Ancient and modern myths of dragon slaying saints* Heart of Albion Press 1993

Index

Other books from
Heart of Albion Press
on Leicestershire and Rutland

VESTIGES OF PAGANISM IN LEICESTERSHIRE
C.J. Billson
Reprint of a classic folklore essay originally published in 1911.
This new edition includes a biography of Billson and annotations to
bring the text up to date. ISBN 1 872883 36 2. 1994, A5, 22 pages,
8 photos, 2 line drawings, card covers. £1.95

STANDING STONES AND MARKSTONES OF
LEICESTERSHIRE AND RUTLAND
Bob Trubshaw
Detailed gazetteer including many newly-rediscovered examples and
rare original illustrations. ISBN 1 872883 02 8. 1991, A5, card
covers, 32pp, 12 illustrations. £1.95

CINEMA IN LEICESTER 1896-1931
David Williams
Thorough research into the early cinemas of the city; fully illustrated.
ISBN 1 872883 20 6. 1993, A5, full colour laminated card cover,
260 pages, 233 illustrations. £12.95

ASFORDBY 1905-1922
MEMORIES OF A LEICESTERSHIRE VILLAGE
John Harold Worley
Detailed and utterly compelling account of growing up in this
fast-changing Leicestershire village during and shortly after the First
World War. With index of the many family names mentioned. ISBN
1 872883 19 2. 1993. A5, laminated card covers, perfect bound, 144
pages, 56 photos, £7.95

AROUND FOXTON
MEMORIES OF AN EDWARDIAN CHILDHOOD
Sarah Dallaston
Highly entertaining reminiscences of growing up at Foxton Locks
before the First World War. With many previously-unpublished
photographs of her life and times. ISBN 1 872883. 1992, A4,
card covers, 38pp, 34 photos £3.50

GRAVE MATTERS
A WALK AROUND WELFORD ROAD CEMETERY,
LEICESTER
Max Wade-Matthews
An irresistible account of Leicester's first cemetery!
A history of its origins with biographies of the many eminent
Victorian and Edwardian Leicester residents buried there.
ISBN 1 872883 12 5. 1992, A5, card covers, 45pp, 36 b&w photos,
12 drawings. £2.95

THE MONUMENTS OF THE CHURCH OF
ST MARY DE CASTRO, LEICESTER
Max Wade-Matthews
A complete transcription of the funeral monuments of this historic church, with brief biographies of many of the more notable persons. ISBN 1 872883 22 2. 1993, A5, card covers, 50 pages, 2 illustrations. £2.95

THE MONUMENTS OF ST NICHOLAS CHURCH
AND ALL SAINTS CHURCH LEICESTER
Max Wade-Matthews
Continuing the series of booklets transcribing the monuments of Leicester's city churches with brief biographies of notable internees. ISBN 1 872883 29 X. 1994, A5, 38 pages, card covers. £2.50

THE MONUMENTS OF ST MARTIN'S CHURCH LEICESTER
Max Wade-Matthews
The most extensive of the series, covering the Cathedral's many notable internments. ISBN 1 872883 30 3. 1994, A5, 76 pages, card covers. £3.95

THE MONUMENTS OF THE CHURCH OF
ST MARGARET, LEICESTER
Max Wade-Matthews
The last of the series covering Leicester's medieval churches. ISBN 1 872883 37 0. A5, 56 pages, card covers. 1995. £3.50

For full catalogue send s.a.e. to:

Heart of Albion Press
2 Cross Hill Close, Wymeswold,
Loughborough, LE12 6UJ
Phone: 01509 880725